WOMAN WITH HAT

WOMAN WITH HAT

LUCY K SHAW

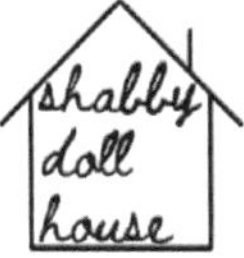

First published by Shabby Doll House
February 2023
www.shabbydollhouse.com
@shabbydollhouse

WOMAN WITH HAT

Set in Bodoni
Cover title set in Bodoni FLF

ISBN: 978-1-7379242-2-7

'I think you have to create the opportunities for yourself. It is not realistic to expect anyone to continue writing in a vacuum. You need people to see and react to your work. So you can start small, with whatever outlets are available to you, or you can join up with friends and publish yourself. In a sense, I'm a self-published writer. All of my full-length books were published by Semiotext(e). At first it was embarrassing, but I realize now it's been a real advantage, being able to figure things out in dialogue with people I trust and respect, and not having to take advice that feels wrong.

\- Chris Kraus

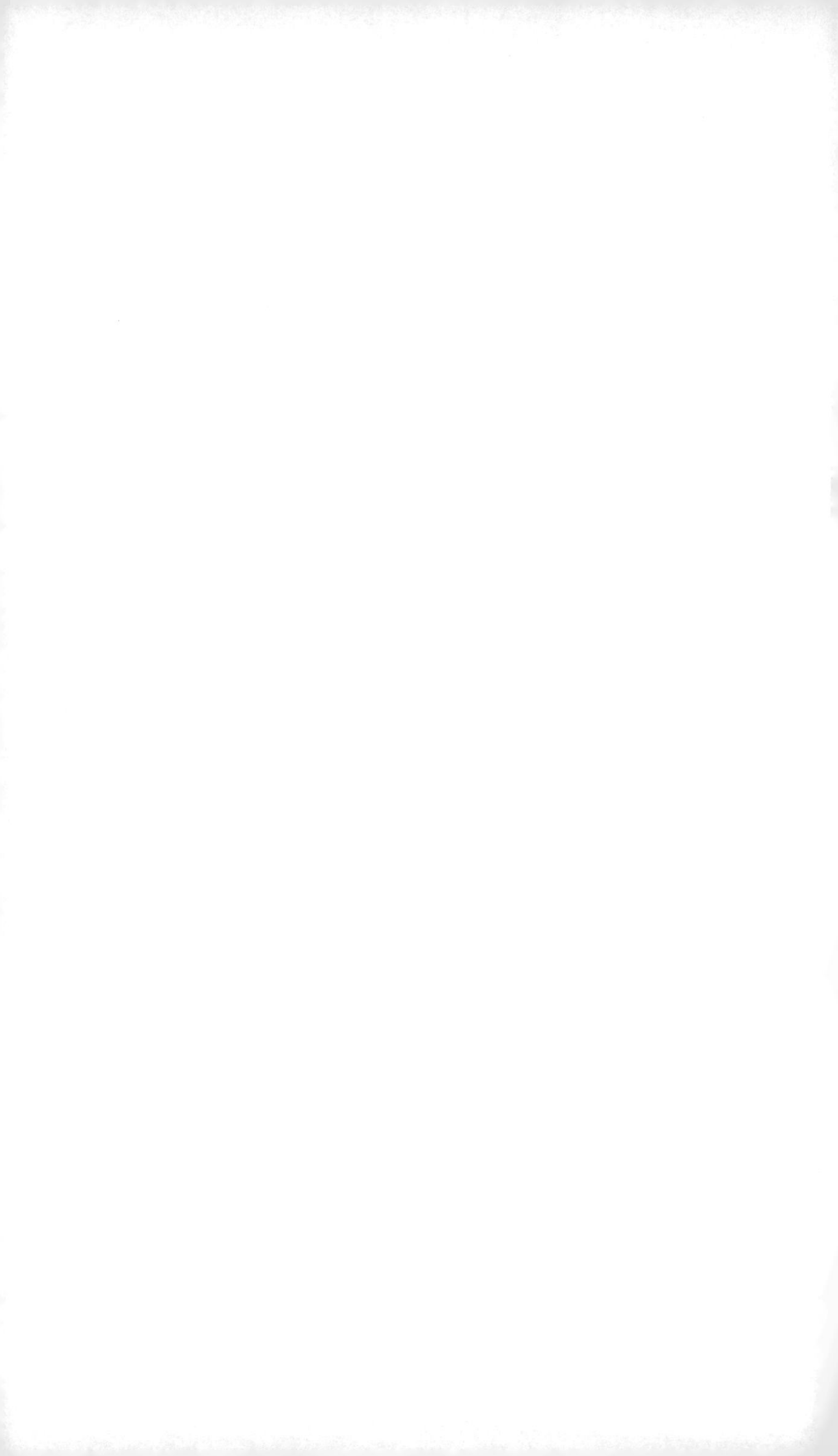

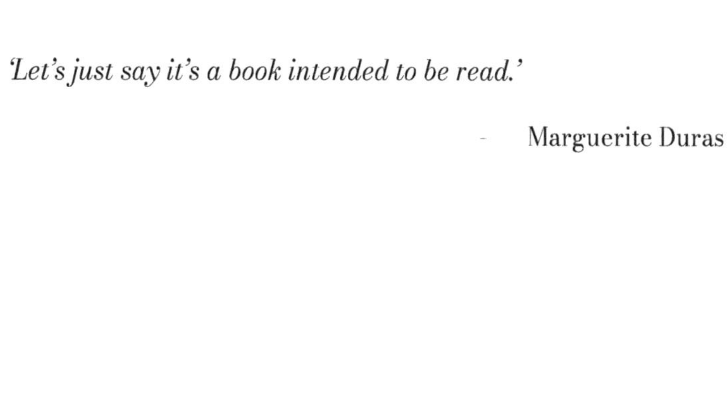

'Let's just say it's a book intended to be read.'

– Marguerite Duras

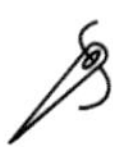

For

E.W.R.C.

WOMAN WITH HAT

1. I need to finish my book, WOMAN WITH HAT, but every time I sit down to write the title piece, WOMAN WITH HAT, I realise I don't have much to add about the well-known 1905 painting by Henri Matisse titled, WOMAN WITH HAT. *(Femme au chapeau)*

2. Instead what I am interested in thinking about is my friend who recently suffered an enormous betrayal.

3. The fragility of the lives we lead and how necessarily we forget it.

4. I don't mean, like, the fact that we could all die at any moment, which is, of course, a given, sure. But rather the idea that we are all supported by and also a part of huge, social, familial ecosystems that we can't even see.

5. And until someone in our inner circle is hurt so brutally by another person in that inner circle, it is impossible to anticipate what that system looks like, how it connects a cast of disparate characters and how far or wide the ripples of one woman's pain could reverberate.

6. The power we have to break each other into pieces.

7. The strength required to keep everybody in place.

8. WOMAN WITH HAT is famous because it became the subject of a scandal at the *salon d'automne* when it was first exhibited in Paris, a hundred and eighteen years ago.

9. One critic went so far as to say that 'a pot of paint had been flung in the face of the public,' which I've always found faintly ridiculous.

10. But actually that's how I feel, now, about my friend's situation.

11. Like a pot of paint has been flung all over her life.

12. And I've got paint in my hair and on my shoes and I'm pissed off.

13. So if you don't know the painting, compositionally, it is a traditional drawing of Henri Matisse's wife, Amélie. However, the brush strokes are loose and clearly visible to the viewer. The choices of colour are non-naturalistic. Green, orange, purple, blue, yellow, red, white, etc.

14. Just like with everything else, I like the story about it most of all. I like the idea that a painting could fuck up everybody's week.

15. But I know the image well because I did an embroidery of its likeness some years ago when I was living in Berlin.

16. Which I suppose I must have sold to somebody, seeing as I don't have it anymore.

17. Perhaps it's on display in the home of someone I've never met, in a place I've never been to.

18. Ecosystems...

19. I didn't think, necessarily, when I started writing this, that these two ideas have any kind of connection. My friend and the painting, WOMAN WITH HAT. They're just what I keep on coming back to. Again, and again.

20. Something about change.

CONVERSATIONALIST

A man sitting on his veranda in Myanmar explains the effects of the military occupation. He tells me that Gen Z are leading the resistance. He says they have formed rebel groups that fight close to the borders. He tells me that the electricity goes on and off every four hours. He says that it is summertime for them, and so hot, it feels like hell. I ask if it is safe for him to talk about it and he tells me, nobody cares anymore. Everybody hates the government. I wish him luck.

A Turkish woman visiting her family in Ankara. She lives in Istanbul and works for a pharmaceutical company. She tells me that everybody takes the train now, instead of driving, because gas prices are so high. She says she loves wine and once visited Bordeaux. She says Turkish wine is very good. She says the grapes are different. Sweet, not dry. She started practising her English at the start of the pandemic because she lived alone and felt so lonely. Two years later, she feels a lot better about her language.

An Egyptian man living in New Cairo, which he tells me is a city established twenty years ago. I tell him that we only really learn about Ancient Egypt, in our culture. I ask him a lot of questions about New Cairo. He says he has lived there for five years. The population is around two million but could eventually reach five. It was developed to alleviate the overcrowding problem in the original Cairo, thirty kilometres away. He likes it. He describes various commercial centres. He says old people and young people live there. All kinds of people. I ask him if it is very international and he says yes there are a lot of immigrants, particularly from Libya.

A Chinese woman I have talked to before and vaguely remember. She is in Shanghai and has been in lockdown for over six weeks, doesn't want to talk about it. Instead she has selected a class entitled 'Famous People' and we discuss attitudes towards fame and celebrity. I teach her some new vocabulary including, *addiction, appearance* and *provided that.* She says she wouldn't want to become famous. She says she is just a normal person. I ask her if writers are celebrated in China and she says, writers are usually like artists, they can become very famous, provided that they're dead.

A Japanese woman who was based in Kuala Lumpur and worked as a flight attendant before the pandemic. Now she is back in Japan and thinking about applying for a working visa for either the UK or Canada. I recommend Canada. She says she is twenty-seven and her friends are starting to get married but she is single. She wants more from her life than they do. But she also worries more than before. What if she can't find a good job? I tell her that she will be fine, because she will have to be fine. I feel connected to her. She seems appreciative. We laugh about hating the men from our respective countries.

A Japanese man who is getting ready for a big meeting tomorrow. He asks if I can look over his plans and correct his choices of vocabulary, but they're already perfect. I have no notes. The meeting is with his boss in Hong Kong. He is proposing some kind of online program to encourage social bonds between employees working from home all over Asia. He has never met any of his co-workers as this is a new job. But he is happy because he can spend more time with his two children. Four and eleven.

A Nepalese woman tells me that she wants to move to the UK but she is very worried about it. She doesn't feel good about her English. There is nobody around for her to practice with. She asks what she can do and I suggest singing along with English music. I ask her about the weather in Nepal and she launches into a description of the landscape. Many mountains. So many mountains.

A Japanese man in his office. A scientific researcher. Today, he says, he has done nothing, but it was still a good day. We talked about the relative prices of various things in different countries. He tells me he likes scuba diving and has scuba dived in Thailand and Australia. I tell him I have snorkelled in Thailand. He says scuba diving is better.

A Chinese woman in Guangzhou tells me she is in the eye of a typhoon right now. And then about her job in social media marketing.

A Chinese man who wants to move to Berlin to study computer science tells me he is not really *an active person.* He graduated last year and lives at home with his parents. He studies English every morning then goes swimming every afternoon. In the evenings he plays computer games with his best friend. He says that his parents do all of the cooking and housework for him. They try to encourage him to learn how to cook but he tells them he doesn't have time to learn. However, he tells me, this isn't true. He does have the time, he just doesn't have the interest.

A German man talks a lot about accents. He wants to master *RP*. He's getting close. He talks about growing up in West Berlin and how it felt crossing the checkpoints into East Germany during his childhood. His family would drive to Austria for vacations. They didn't have a lot of money. The car would break down. It was a twenty-five-year-old car. The police would stop his family and suspect them of people smuggling. Very, very unpleasant, he remembers. It is not a bad thing if the youth don't understand, he says. Because even now, he thinks of those times very often. Every time he passes where the checkpoint used to be. Not far from his home.

OBSERVATIONS IN ABSENTIA

1. The absence of scrolling (this is a huge one).

2. My fingers would move to open the apps without my consent (but they had gone).

3. I have no idea what anyone is doing.

4. I don't need to know what anyone is doing.

5. I want to know though about some people.

6. Although the idea of keeping up an individual correspondence with every person I know seems unrealistic.

7. Blogging?

8. What is this thing where we announce our lives to each other? It's not a conversation.

9. Although I miss the friends I don't talk to much, only observe, (particularly in other languages).

10. Is it artistic? Writing about my life over photos that I've taken?

11. (Yes, of course).

12. Is it cruel? Are we permanently damaged? Addicted actually?

13. (It feels possible.)

14. Reading a lot about the ways the apps are designed.

15. Reading the news a lot. (Replacing.)

16. Duolingo French and Spanish every day to fill some gaps.

17. I don't know what 'everyone' thinks about Russia/Ukraine/Partygate... I have to come up with my own ideas.

18. Nobody reaches out to ask if I'm okay, which is fine (in this case, because I am) but there are many people I don't talk to.

19. Caroline brings a cat to book club and I'm surprised.

20. Book sales are down.

21. I feel aware that there's a character of me, that I created, with a certain aesthetic, and a certain tone, but it's a relief not to have to write for her.

22. Narratives...

23. The first few days felt strange, then like a holiday, then like I wanted to go home and see everybody, and then like I just forgot about it, mostly.

24. Everyone seems to have a strategy.

25. Delete from your phone, don't look before bed, airplane mode at night, don't look in the mornings, use a screen time app to track your other apps, only look on the computer.

26. Okay but why?

27. Definitely the sleeping is better!

28. Maybe even a little happier.

29. There's something about the pandemic and our renewed reliance on technology... Maybe a month away has helped me to process it all a little bit, taken me out of it.

30. I've also been in an empty surf town in the south of Spain this whole time.

31. Do I want to go back?

32. Yeah.

33. I mean, I want to be more intentional, conscious, catch myself before a mindless scroll, not reach for it unthinkingly.

34. Use it as a tool to serve my goals, (you know, probably doing some kind of writing thing).

35. But I need to look less.

36. Revolutionise my relationship to it...

37. (I didn't even feel like there was a problem before this).

38. Now I would recommend some time away to anybody.

39. When I redownloaded Instagram this morning and scrolled through the stories: X person had moved away, Y person was in Mexico, Z person was sharing screenshots of some theories about vaccine mandates, there was someone I met at a wedding once...

40. Maybe some kind of blogging is a good idea, actually.

41. There is, after all, this need to communicate.

ALICE NOTLEY Y LA PLAYA

Okay I'm sitting here with a gin and tonic after my second ever surf lesson and I'm writing because I have things to share. I want to tell somebody my thoughts about this Alice Notley interview that I relistened to over the past couple of days.

I listened between the classes I was teaching, while I was making breakfast, etc. And I also listened to it a year ago, alone in my apartment, while I was painting furniture. The way she asserts herself makes me feel emboldened and I love it.

I want to share a couple of quotes:

'Poetry is for reading. You just sit down with a book and read it. You don't have to beat your head against the wall about it. You just read it.'

Yes!

'Pleasure's good, and it isn't emphasised enough in the way people talk about poetry, but it isn't important to talk about what poetry does, I mean, we know that there's poetry, we know that we want this art. It's a really ancient art. It's not going away. It's completely

necessary to us, even if we have the most minuscule culture. We still need it. The conversation about what it is is ridiculous.'

I'm smiling and my face is hot.

Surfing is really intense and I want to do it forever.

Though I also feel nostalgic for this time last year when we read *Autobiography of Red* by Anne Carson and *The Descent of Alette* by Alice Notley and *If Not, Winter* by Sappho in the book club, and I had all of that time to learn everything about those authors and books and to sink really deep into them, even if I didn't understand them or like them at first, because I couldn't do anything else, like learn how to surf, or go outside after the 6pm curfew.

What are we going to read this year? What are we going to learn?

When I listen to Alice Notley talk about her work, I feel excited to live a long life of writing things that nobody asked for.

Wow, my face is really alive with heat!

(Sunburn.)

Okay, one more quote from the interview now:

'I don't advocate anything. I think people should stop working so hard at their jobs and stop earning so much

money and stop being interested in objects and just take it easy, read a few poems.'[1]

Okay, me too.

[1] Search 'Alice Notley interview' on YouTube. It's the one with the picture of her whole face.

WAR MONGERING

I often think about something this guy Jack said seventeen years ago, we were at sixth form college talking on the side of the road between classes, we weren't exactly friends (though we had some in common), so it was unusual for us to stop to chat, he was always so pretentious, always wearing a scarf, which really said something at the time, however that morning there had been a series of bombings in central London, three explosions on the underground and another on a double decker bus, it had happened just before 9 o'clock when commuters would have been heading to work, and we were on our way to college, so none of us had seen the news, didn't really understand exactly what had happened or might still be happening, a lot of rumours were swirling around, and everybody was scared, remember this was only four years after 9/11, so when I ran into Jack on the side of the road we exchanged information about whatever we'd heard, fifty something people had been killed, I reported, and he seemed a little disappointed, made a face I didn't understand, and then I remember him saying, 'We all secretly want things like this to be worse than they actually are, we all want to see what could happen.'

WOMAN WITH HAT 2

1. Feels absurd that I wake up and have to shuffle to the bathroom in fear that I've leaked blood all over the bed sheets and when I get there, I have to pull a plastic cup out of me and empty its contents into the toilet.

2. I guess I have another month to myself in this body.

3. And all the while, he is still asleep. He looks so beautiful when he is asleep.

4. I like to wake up and write though. The potential leaking has forced me to my computer.

5. I like to walk through to the living room and open the windows and the shutters wide and feel the cooler air from out there mixing with the warmer air from in here. I like to make my maté drink and get under the blanket on the sofa and lean back.

6. I was reading Joe Brainard last night before bed. I have the collected works of Joe Brainard and the collected works of Oscar Wilde lying next to each other on the floor beside me. I have an embroidery I finished yesterday because I was procrastinating on writing. Or I couldn't write because my period was causing me too much pain. Or I knew that

everything I was thinking wasn't what I really think.

7. I read *The Red Zone* by Chloe Caldwell earlier this summer and it taught me to be kinder to myself when I'm menstruating.

8. Now I'm hoping that the upswing in oestrogen that I'm going to experience over the next two weeks will give me the energy I need to finally finish this collection.

9. It's hard to stop writing it though. Every time I see another friend, I feel inspired to tell another story.

10. Over the past few weeks, I have reunited with a couple of people I hadn't seen since before the pandemic started. Two people I've known for a long time, and love to spend time with. Two people who live far away.

11. Two friends, from different countries, different marriages, who have gotten divorced since I last saw them.

12. Two friends who introduced me to their new partners, told me their new stories, demonstrated their new ways of living, and glowed.

THE CHRONICLE OF TAIF

Every Thursday evening, Hussain Kamal drives the two hours back from Jeddah, where he works, to Taif, where he lives. The heat in Jeddah is very intense. 35 degrees in December. But inland, in the mountains, he can walk around comfortably in the evenings. He can visit the barber's shop wearing a polo shirt that says TOUGH across his chest.

He likes driving. Whenever he wants to think, he goes for a drive. Where, it doesn't matter. He just wants to be moving. If he stays still, he wants to go to sleep. But when he's driving, he wants to think about his life. He can access some kind of clarity. He can weave his way through the traffic and see himself from without.

On the highway, he opens the English learning app and scrolls through the available teachers. Unconsciously, he clicks on the picture of a dark haired, white girl: Sarah.

'Sarah, I like your name,' he tells her. 'Sarah is Arabic name.'

(It is not really her name but she says thank you anyway.)

Sarah asks him where he's going and about his day. She asks him where he lives, and he begins his story. He was born in Palestine, his citizenship is Jordanian, but he's been living in Saudi Arabia for seventeen years. A lot of people live in Saudi Arabia for work, he says.

She doesn't ask about his work and he doesn't try to tell her.

He navigates the traffic as they make small talk, his phone supported by a holder on the dashboard. He explains the geography of the region, the climate, etc.

She tells him that she lives in France but that she is originally from England and he asks her, *which is better*?

It's not exactly the question he wants to ask, and she knows that.

What he means is, what are the differences, and why did you go there?

But she fumbles over some explanation about the culture, the food, the language, and in the meantime, he parks his car, having arrived back in Taif.

Are you married? He asks her, point blank.

Yes, my husband is French, she tells him, clearly marking herself as unavailable he understands, while doubting that she is telling the truth.

Any children? He asks.

No, she says. What about you?

And that's when he really gets going. He has four children, three boys and a girl. Another one on the way. In three months. He will be another boy.

Congratulations, she tells him.

About their ages: The oldest is sixteen and his little girl is three.

I'm thirty, he jokes.

Oh, so cute, says Sarah, ignoring him.

There is a big age gap between the oldest and the youngest.

Yes, I got married when I was twenty-four, he tells her. And there was one more child too.

But he died.

Oh? She says, unprepared.

He was in an accident.

What happened?

He was playing football and the ball was kicked into the road...

Oh no...

And he went to get the ball and...

Oh no...

There was an accident and he died.

Oh no.

Sarah was so terribly sorry.

As Hussein had expected.

He told her about how difficult it had been because he had no family in Saudi Arabia. They all live in Palestine and Jordan. It was just him and his wife and his remaining children.

When did this happen? Sarah asked him.

About two years ago, Hussein told her.

At the start of the pandemic...

Could anybody come to visit?

Yes, they came after two or three days, but it was difficult for anybody to enter Saudi Arabia.

Hussein had gotten out of the car and was now walking down a quiet street.

Where are you now? Sarah asked.

I am walking in the district, he said, the district of my barber's.

What time is it in Saudi Arabia? Sarah asked him, knowing full well what time it was in Saudi Arabia.

It is about 9pm, he told her.

And you can go to the barber's shop at 9pm?

Yes, he will open until 12am. Everybody works in the evenings here because it is too hot during the day.

HERE'S WHAT YOU NEED TO KNOW AFTER DAY FOUR OF THE WAR

1. I get these glimpses into my disconnection.

2. Some girls are speaking French on the path by the river during my afternoon walk, and I feel surprised.

3. Until I remember that I live in France.

4. I look across the street into my neighbour's apartment as I'm going to bed and when I notice the lights are on, begin to calculate what time it is over there.

5. It's too late.

A DECADE UNDER THE INFLUENCE

I'm writing on the train from Paris to Nevers, where I haven't been for two months. I spent Christmas and New Year in England, and then the next six weeks on the south-west coast of Spain, working and walking along the beach every day.

It's strange to be back in France, with the three languages mixing together in my mind, and even some German thrown in too. There were a lot of German people in the town where we stayed.

'Los alemanes quieren el sol' said some lady in a hallway.

'Estamos lo mismo,' admitted Chris.

In Andalusia, the sky was bright blue and the light was so incredible and you could see so far in every direction when you were on the beach that I had to take off my sunglasses sometimes to remind myself that it was real.

Picture me: I'm running in the morning and I'm listening to a podcast and I'm surrounded by absolutely nothing.

Picture me as though from a drone.

Here the sky hangs heavy and grey, there are no leaves on the trees. The ground is dark and everything looks damp.

It doesn't seem to make sense that both things could be happening at the same time.

That it's possible to travel between such different landscapes within a couple of hours.

That we, as a people, can fly?

And yet I, as an individual, am so simple...

I went back onto social media after a month without looking at it, but it started to feel something like drinking a Monster energy drink and eating a bag of Haribo sour mix at the same time, so I haven't been looking at it much since my return. I become aware of myself being sucked into a disgusting-feeling scroll almost immediately, and then I'm repulsed by it. The layouts of the apps feel clunky and chaotic now that I've untrained my eyes from looking at them.

I was ready to get back into active participation but now the thrill is gone.

So I'm ready for a new mode of communicating. Hence why I started writing this.

I love writing for my own amusement.

Putting these words together, just to play.

Talking to nobody.

Making myself laugh...

Oh, one thing I keep meaning to mention to somebody, but so far have kept to myself:

This month marks ten years since I started working on Shabby Doll House.

Ten years since I had the idea to make some kind of magazine and bought *shabbydollhouse.com*...

Kind of an interesting fact.

I feel like I should be invited somewhere to stand in front of a podium to give a rousing speech about how I changed the world.

I do, on some level, really think that.

And I suppose I could just write the speech here in this book...

But no, I will wait patiently for my invitation from whoever owns a podium.

And then I will say no, sorry!

I don't want or need your institutional support!

Thank you, but no thank you.

And then, and only then, will I post the speech in full, on the Shabby Doll House website, so that people can read it alone at their computers, the way Shabby Doll House was intended to be experienced, by God.

Just kidding, God is not, nor has ever been, an editor of Shabby Doll House.

Or, in my humble opinion, ever existed in any capacity!

Anyway.

I just wanted to take myself for a nice little walk.

Thank you for joining me.

Where shall we go next time?

Ah, I just looked out of the window and saw the river Loire.

And then I actually said out loud, Ahhhhh!

On returning to the place where I wrote a whole novel last year, I can't help but feel like the protagonist.

TIME CAPSULE

Close friends only: a meme featuring, I think, the man from *Curb Your Enthusiasm*, which I have never seen.

A shared post on 'the new NYC teacher contract negotiations.'

An advertisement in French for the aperitif, *Lillet.*

A screenshot of a friend's newly released single being featured on a playlist of new indie music.

A photo of the Croatian bartender I befriended at Sam and Brian's wedding, as a child, wearing some kind of prom dress.

An acquaintance standing in front of a big blank canvas, holding up a paint brush, wearing heavy duty trousers and a bikini top.

An advertisement for a swimsuit company.

A close-up of some kind of unfamiliar green fruit with a sticker on it that says '*Limelon.*'

A video of something like a table being drilled together, from above, with the caption 'Be Your Own Butch.'

A selfie of someone wearing a mask and looking bored at work with the devil horns filter on.

The back cover of a book that recently came out.

An advertisement for a company selling expensive-looking rings.

A photo of a hipster Muslim woman sitting in front of some cacti.

A photo of a 12th century castle in Italy where some people who just got engaged are staying.

An advertisement for *PrimeVideoFR*.

The front cover of a new book that recently came out.

A shared post about a short story just published online.

The inside pages of a French book with one sentence, half visible, highlighted in green.

A shared post in Romanian for a poetry anthology I am to be included in.

An advertisement for some kind of jewellery company.

A meme about how it's okay to struggle with motherhood.

A photo of somebody having a smoothie bowl in Los Angeles.

A shared post of a creepy 1904 painting by Maximilian Lenz called 'Spring.'

An advertisement for what seems like a new phone company but it's unclear.

Available tattoo appointments in July by a friend who recently moved to Berlin.

A video about a deck someone is building in Portland.

An advertisement for Tiffany's.

A photo of a dish someone is cooking that appears to include carrots, onions, parsley and indistinguishable animal flesh.

An advertisement for some perfume.

A meme featuring a tired looking furby sitting at a breakfast table accompanied by a toy mouse.

A meme featuring a fish eating a fibre-optic cable, which means absolutely nothing to me although I recognise having seen it before.

An advertisement for bronzer.

A poster for an opening reception at an art school in Los Angeles tomorrow.

A photograph of a quilt from the Cook Islands.

A meme about managing a bar.

An advertisement for some supposedly flattering shorts.

A sketch of some strawberries from the New Yorker accompanied by a joke I don't bother to read.

A photo of someone's mom who died.

A poem about queer friendships.

An advertisement from *Le Grand Est* region of France asking me to fight against illegal waste dumps?

A poster for the Bucharest Film Awards.

Footage from a live concert by someone I don't recognise.

An advertisement for a beige t-shirt with the words BRAINS ARE THE NEW TITS written across the chest.

EMBROIDERY IDEA

I was running from Conil de la Frontera to El Palmar de Vejer one evening in May with my new friend Mahshid.

Mahshid does the same kind of yoga as Chris, which is why we all found ourselves in this specific town in the south-west of Spain when we met each other in January.

When we came back to visit a few months later, Mahshid told me that she had also started running and she was doing one of those training programs where you run for a minute, walk for a minute, that kind of thing. So I said that I would like to go with her.

I'm fascinated by running and my personal experience of it. I think it's one of the most interesting and fulfilling things in my life. But when I try to write about it, or even talk about it, it doesn't really transfer.

Nonetheless I have an idea for a story. Or two.

Conil is a small town about an hour south of Cadiz. The beach there is very wide, very beautiful and very, very windy.

About halfway between Conil and the next town, El Palmar, there is a large, 13th century stone tower. The tower was originally part of some kind of defence fortress and then later, I suppose in calmer times, used as a lookout point for viewing migrating schools of tuna as they passed by during the so-called tuna season. The sight of it is a constant when you're in the area. A bizarre, ancient, man-made structure penetrating the blue sky.

That evening, the light was so bright and beautiful. It was breath-taking. We were all preparing to move on to other locations in the coming days and I felt as though I wanted to hold onto the landscape for as long as I could.

So here I am, writing to you about it.

Mahshid's running program required that we walk for a few minutes first to warm up before we started to run, and as we did this, Mahshid warned me repeatedly that she was very new to running and that I was not to look at her while she was doing it.

I assured her this would not be a problem.

To me, one of the greatest parts of running is being able to run with a friend. And one of the greatest parts of running with a friend is that you get the opportunity to engage in a long, one-on-one conversation without any distractions, and without ever looking one another in the eye.

Something opens up inside of you when you're running alongside someone and speaking.

That is, once you reach the stage at which you can run and speak easily at the same time without struggling to breathe, which, of course, takes a lot of practice.

So we started. The terrain is a sandy trail that runs parallel with the sea. Run one minute. Walk one minute. Run two minutes, etc. I don't remember the exact details. Mahshid just told me what to do and when. We started talking about our plans for the summer. I told her about where I had been in the interim months since we had last seen each other. I asked her about how she felt to be leaving this place and going on to Hungary and then India. And I noted that the more we ran, the more difficult it was becoming for her to respond comfortably. After one of my questions she signalled that she would answer during the next walking period and we both laughed.

As we ran past the tower and on towards El Palmar, I offered to Mahshid that I could tell her a story in order to distract her and she accepted.

Now I will tell that story to you too.

RUNNING STORY NUMBER ONE

At the end of January, 2020, I travelled back to England at a few hours' notice because we thought that my nana's death was imminent.

But then, after I arrived, prepared for the worst, she just kept on living.

The doctors told us that she was dying, but they didn't know how long it would take. Maybe a few weeks or months.

I didn't need to be anywhere else, so it didn't make sense to go anywhere else. I couldn't just say goodbye, knowing I would be back soon for her funeral.

Though, at the same time, it felt strange to put my life on hold like that, because my life had, up until then, been so much up to me.

However, I wasn't the only one in limbo and that made it easier. My sister, who had been living in China, had also come home quite suddenly, and so we were both there together, not wanting to go or knowing how long to stay.

My family live in a little village in the Yorkshire countryside. I grew up in the city nearby. But my parents moved when I was in my early twenties and I like it. It's beautiful like in the David Hockney paintings and I can go home without having to see anyone else I know from growing up, which is ideal.

As usual, when I was at home, or anywhere, I suppose, I went running several times a week. I would wake up early in the morning and go out before I started teaching online. I would run around the village, do 'the village loop' as we call it. It is only a short distance, a total of about 4km, but it was the only route I knew in the area at the time.

A few days into my stay there, to my surprise, my mum expressed an interest in running too. There had been a local beginners running group that started after New Year's Day, and she had toyed with attending it before deciding that it was too cold and too daunting. But she brought it up a couple of times noncommittally, that she wished that she could run too. So when Chris came out to join us in the house of hospital visits a few days after I arrived, I asked him to bring my other pair of running shoes. My old ones. My mum and I wear the same size. And then we downloaded the '*Couch to 5k*' application and decided we would set off at 8am the following morning.

Which, by the way, was a big deal. My mum was 58 years old at the time and hadn't run since P.E class. And my sister, who we guilted into joining us, was less than enthusiastic also.

'Couch to 5k' is a training program very similar to the one that Mahshid was trying, which is why I suppose I brought it up with her.

It consists of nine weeks of podcasts in which the enthusiastic voice of a minor celebrity tells you when to stop and when to start and, most importantly, encourages you to keep going.

It started out ostensibly painlessly, like, walk for five minutes to warm up and then run for one minute, and then walk for two minutes etc... But the first whole minute of running is the scariest sixty seconds in the entire programme for people who haven't run before.

Once you get past that part, it gets easier.

You complete the same training session three times and then you move onto the next week's challenge. And obviously, with each week it becomes a little more difficult.

We would wake up and meet in the living room at 8am. Start running as the roads defrosted and the sun came up. The sky burning orange as the daylight broke through the winter mornings. We were walking and we were running and we were talking. You know, I guess it was mostly me who was talking. My mum would be wearing a hat and a scarf and some gloves and maybe by the end she would have removed the gloves. But we would all feel good and we would all feel cold. And I would tell them stories to distract them as they moved through the morning. And then later we would visit Nana and we would tell her about what we had done and she would act as surprised and impressed as she did, honestly, about everything that we ever did. And she would say, "*Keep running, Jane.*" Jane is my mum's name. "*Keep running while you're still young.*"

I have written before about visiting Nana in that care home. But I will write about it again because it was one of the more important moments of my life and this is my book.

I think it made us feel a lot better about everything during that time. The running that we did together every other morning. Nana was dying in the care home, we were all stuck in the house together, and there was this thing happening, this pandemic looming, that we really had no understanding of. No idea of what was coming next.

Over the course of a few weeks, my mum went from struggling to run for one minute, to being able to keep going for five and then ten and soon fifteen minutes.

The mornings became lighter, even warmer. She didn't need her scarf anymore. Started taking off her hat.

When we started the nine-week program, we said there's no way that we'll ever be able to complete this together. I expected to be long gone before then.

But around five weeks into the program we got put into the first lockdown.

It still seems unbelievable.

My sister and I deleted everything except FaceTime from an old iPad that week, while we were still allowed to enter the care home. We left it with the nurses so that they could call us in case we couldn't visit.

For a few days, visitors were still allowed, even in spite of the restrictions to do anything else. They would take your temperature at the door. Two people maximum. Then they cut it down to one person. And finally, nobody could go at all.

How strange that I had rushed back to England only a few weeks earlier, thinking that she was going to die at any minute. And now the whole world had changed immeasurably. But she was still here.

I don't remember the last time I saw her.

Or maybe I do. I have a memory of leaving her room, waving and smiling and saying goodbye, with her doing the same thing in my direction, before popping my head back around the door a few seconds later and seeing her lying there in the bed looking absolutely miserable.

I didn't mean to catch her like that. I thought she was expecting me to look back. But she didn't. And she had been performing.

Performing life.

Performing strength.

It might not have been the last time. In fact, I don't think it was. But I can't remember the last time. When somebody is dying, you think every time will be the last time and then you lose track.

Anyway, we kept on running.

When the prime minister appeared on TV and told us that we would have to stay at home for three weeks, we couldn't believe it. Three weeks! We thought that was implausible.

But the weeks just kept on passing.

Spring came into bloom.

We got closer and closer to the nine week finish line. To the day when we would have to run for over thirty minutes together. No walking. No warm-up. Just waking up and going.

Nana died a few days before we finished the 5km challenge.

One evening the phone rang and my mum answered, and a nurse told her that Nana had died.

My sister started sobbing.

Chris and I were eating dinner at the table, and my immediate reaction was relief. I was relieved that she didn't have to be alone in the care home, confused as to why nobody was visiting her anymore.

She had been on FaceTime just a few hours earlier.

She had received a birthday card from my aunt that wished her a happy 90th birthday.

And we think that this is when she gave up on living, when she thought that she had made it to a new decade, when she thought that she had equalled her own mother's age.

She didn't. She died six days early. But it doesn't matter.

A few days later, on her birthday, we ran the last run of the Couch to 5k program.

'Keep running while you're still young.'

The night before, my sister and I designed and printed out a certificate and placed it into a gold frame.

This Certifies that Jane Shaw has completed the Couch to 5km challenge.

Head Coach: Lucy K Shaw

Assistant Coach: Kate Shaw

We prepared a closing ceremony which involved orange juice poured into champagne flutes.

We gave Chris and my dad a dressing gown cord and asked them to come outside at a certain time, to hold it up as a finishing line for her to run through at the end of the challenge. We even filmed it.

And the truth is that nothing I write can capture the emotion clearly visible in that six second video.

The details are too small.

And I'm sure I missed a lot of this when I was telling it to Mahshid too. Except for that it will have come across in my voice, as I was running.

I wanted to write this down because it's a story about how running has helped me and helped other people when we needed it.

Instead of wallowing in bed that morning, a few days after Nana died, we were out running in the sunshine, completing something. Accomplishing the impossible.

A 58-year-old orphan running 5km for the first time in her life.

When I think about the images that I want to embroider, I tend to linger on a photo of a scene that felt really important and that I want to remember. But sometimes it's not possible to contain just within stitches. I need words.

This was embroidery idea number one.

I wonder what it looks like to you.

IN THIS HOUSE WE BELIEVE

1. Meat is murder.
2. Cheese is labour.
3. Dinner should be served after 9pm.
4. Ketchup is an insult.
5. Hong Kong is a country.
6. Self-publishing is empowering.
7. Sex and the City is the great American novel.
8. Red wine should be served chilled.
9. Everyone must shower between swimming in the river and getting into bed.
10. Hanging clothes out to dry in the wind on a blustery morning is one of life's most underrated pleasures.

REIMAGINING ALEKSANDR PETROVSKY

human or machine?

1 year ago

I never found him particularly alluring, but as I get older, I'm increasingly attracted to him for his calm demeanour, creative mind, good taste, sophistication, and worldliness.

bbria28

5 years ago

He is so handsome but I think he would intimidate me.

Pamela Reyes

6 years ago

he was by far my favorite character, I would totally date him, he so serious that is sexy

Natalie Hamilton

4 weeks ago

I was young and foolish when I watch this for first time! He's so charming

Liz Clegg

3 months ago

He is quite rude. He was rude to Charlotte when he first met her and Carrie. And he sarcastically says congratulations when she tells him she's a writer.

JustynaSitko

6 months ago

He doesn't believe in "When in Rome, do as the Romans". He thinks his culture is superior to the American way of things. He must like Carrie just for her looks as he seems not to appreciate her intelligence and sense of humor. He thinks Americans are ignorants, but by acting this way he shows lack of good manners and comes of as ignorant himself.

Krissy S

3 years ago

Hes a typical artist and she is clearly out of her depth culturally. Fitting though that she got vodka

Paula Galloway

6 years ago

Even in his advanced age, he is... magnetic.

Mandira Improta

7 months ago
I would go CRAZY for a man like that !!!!

AnimalCrossingStoryMaker
2 years ago

Omg he is absolutely not my type, but maybe I'm just to young hahaha

CobraDove

5 months ago (edited)

I would not be attracted to him at all...it's cringey, his poem reading

Lori Crockett-Owens

4 years ago

OMG. When Alexander starts talking about his art. Lol I feel that way sometimes when I draw.

What if it's not enough... I feel ya, Alexander.

Gabriel Bolaños Hernández

3 years ago

Any body knows where can I find the scene in where he sweeten tea with black cherries

Lee249

7 months ago

Speaking from my younger selfish immature stance. I always believed that Petrovsky was too obsessed about his Art Career than to spare Carrie's feelings for happiness. My opinion have changed since.

ekunsa

1 year ago (edited)

We Europeans are really different from simple Americans

Calvin Bethea

1 year ago

This was just bad writing. Carrie who is a writer and supposedly this quirky free spirit has never dated any type of artist who created for her. She preferred a date at McDonalds to a night at The Met. I would not expect that lack of sophistication from a would be journalist living in New York of her age.

CYBR ANGEL

4 years ago

$9.54 for all that food? Wow... i miss those days lol now the quarter pounder alone is like $7 and the chicken nuggets start at $6

writerspen010

6 years ago

Carrie, if you don't want this older, worldly man with whom you can discuss literature, poetry, and opera, I'll gladly take him, and your theatre tickets, off your hands

lucykshaw

1 hour ago (edited)

So for me, it's not really about whether or not I find Aleksandr Petrovsky attractive. I don't, I suppose. But rather, I think, it's that I want to be Aleksandr Petrovsky. I want to be a self-assured, multi-lingual, world-renowned artist who flits from New York to Paris to Saint Petersburg, or wherever. I mean, I am a little like this already, without the fame or the money. But yeah, I found myself, during my most recent rewatch of the entire six seasons of *Sex and the City*, (I am finally about the same age as the characters were during the show) feeling like I had culturally outgrown Carrie and company. I mean, there are plenty of ways in which I don't feel that way. Their relationship to wealth, and their unquestioning, dominant position within their own society, for example, felt as unattainable as ever. But for most of the show, you only ever really see these characters in their comfort zones. And it is really interesting, when they introduce this Petrovsky character, how shallow and uncultured they begin to seem. How quickly they feel out of their depth as soon as they meet somebody from another country. Was that how the average New Yorker acted in the early 2000s? Surely not. But then again? It's like they regress into their Americanness. I mean, since when has Carrie ever eaten at McDonald's? That does really feel like lazy writing. But beyond that, she finds it embarrassing when he wants to dance with her? She cringes when he reads her a poem? She laughs at the conceptual artist they see together? I mean... She's supposed to be a writer? But she doesn't appreciate or even strive to understand art? Okay, I guess I know people like this. Perhaps I have even been like this. But when she goes to Paris with him, aged 36, it's as though she's the first person in the history of the world to travel overseas. She doesn't make any plans for herself and then feels annoyed that he's always working... towards the opening of his first solo exhibition in six years...

Anyway, my favourite scene and something that I really find myself coming back to again and again, is Aleksandr Petrovsky's gothic dinner party, which takes place at his apartment in Manhattan before their fateful trip to Paris. In this sequence, we see the whole cast together, which is rare. Even Stanford and Marcus are invited. Samantha is there with Smith. Charlotte and Miranda bring their husbands, Harry and Steve. There is a real grown up feeling to the group. We're so used to seeing just the four women together, and then suddenly we see them as this whole ensemble. Carrie's voiceover opens the scene with the oddly specific idea that, '*For most women, the goal of a dinner party is to have your friends feel comfortable around their boyfriend.*' And it quickly becomes apparent that, in our contemporary vernacular, the vibes are off. Carrie's friends are loud and crass. Samantha tells a xenophobic story about how she thinks her maid is using her vibrator. Steve compliments Aleksandr's piano and asks if he knows any Billy Joel. Aleksandr, who is dressed all in black at the head of the table, looking completely vampiric, is unfamiliar. Charlotte asks him about his sculptures for the upcoming show. Carrie corrects her, they're actually large-scale light installations integrated with video imagery. Aleksandr doesn't want to talk about it. The subject moves on to Paris and this idea that Carrie might be moving there with him, at which point everybody else around the table looks aghast. Aleksandr says that Paris is the greatest city in the world. Harry says he hates Paris. Nobody feels comfortable around Carrie's boyfriend, the well-established goal of any woman's dinner party. And I couldn't help but wonder what Aleksandr himself thinks about all of this. Do he and Carrie discuss the awkward tension later, after their guests have gone home? Or do they just gloss over it, pretending that it never happened?

For what it's worth, and I don't think it's much, I can deeply relate to the expressions on Aleksandr Petrovsky's face when he is trying not to openly express disapproval at the quality of the group's conversation but is also obviously incapable of pretending he feels otherwise. I know that I can be Petrovsky-esque in this sense, way more often than I'd prefer to be.

And when I watch this scene, I understand that I'm supposed to be viewing him as cold and rude and foreign. But I actually find myself empathising with him, in his severity and self-seriousness. I too want to have big, gothic dinner parties where the guests talk about art and philosophy in multiple languages and feel intellectually matched. That's just me.

What am I doing? It's 2:36 in the morning and I'm sitting up in the dark writing a fake YouTube comment in response to a specific scene from a TV show that aired eighteen years ago. I need to stop. I do have a lot of thoughts about the differences between European and American cultures, but I only really know a few people and I don't want to offend all of them.

All I know tonight, is that people have been talking, for over twenty years, about whether they're a Carrie or a Miranda or a Charlotte or a Samantha. And I've never really felt like any of them. Or recognised an alternative option, until now...

Man, I feel like Aleksandr Petrovsky.

POWERPUFF GIRLS

It was at the end of a long weekend spent upstate at the wedding of a great friend. We were sitting in the living room of the house we had rented for the occasion. I had been up for hours, still jet-lagged after flying in from Paris a few days earlier. Ashley had emerged, ready to go, at the dining table, while I was out eating breakfast. And then Rachelle wandered into the room wearing a t-shirt dress that she had sported at various points throughout the weekend and presumably had slept in.

The last time we had been together, perhaps eight hours earlier, we were sitting around a fire pit after coming home from the wedding party and everyone, it seemed to me at the time, was more wasted than I was. (I was considerably wasted.) There had been this beautiful moment, packed into the back of the taxi home, when they were all leaning backwards, looking up at the stars and aww-ing.

So, now everyone was hungover.

When I woke up, calves aching from the dance party, and came upstairs to sit on the sofa at around 8 o'clock, it occurred to me that I should have done something to record this momentous occasion. The reunion, after a global pandemic, of three iconic literary women: Rachelle Toarmino, Ashley Obscura and... me.

Our DIY publishing outfits, Peach Mag, Metatron Press and Shabby Doll House, have published poems and stories and pictures and books by countless people from all over the world, which is cool and strange and possible in part because of wilful determination, in part because of the internet, and in part because of each other.

So I wrote some questions on my phone that I planned to ask them before our noon checkout. I was hoping we would have time to get something to eat together, maybe we could sit at the diner on the corner, and I could press record, start a conversation. But then nobody else got up, so I went for breakfast without them. (Florentine omelette, I copied Rachelle's order from the day before.) And when I came back, Ashley told me she was leaving soon, waiting to be picked up and driven to New York.

Enter Rachelle into the living room.

So I asked them, out of nowhere, it must have seemed, if I might ask them a few questions and if they would mind being recorded for a vague project I was working on, which they graciously, for some reason, accepted.

HOW DO ARTISTS SURVIVE?

Rachelle: Either rich parents or...

(laughing)

Ashley: I would say community...

Rachelle: Other artists. I don't think I would keep doing it if I didn't have friends also doing it right now. Or I'm sure we'd still write but I don't think I'd be as excited about doing it or get as energised by doing it if other people weren't doing it too.

Ashley: Same.

WE ARE FAMOUSLY THE POWERPUFF GIRLS OF INTERNET LITERATURE... SHABBY DOLL HOUSE, PEACH MAG, METATRON PRESS, ETC. BUT MY QUESTION IS, WHY US? WHY DID WE DO THAT?

Rachelle: Because we're girls.

Ashley: Because we're amazing women who have good organisational skills.

(laughter)

And maybe because we didn't have the community we wanted. I feel like all the projects we started were just a means to create community around us.

And we're obviously crazy.

HOW DO WE FEEL AT THIS TIME IN OUR LIVES?

Rachelle: I'm so hungover.

(laughter)

Ashley: I am also incredibly hungover, but I honestly feel like I'm so happy right now. It hasn't been like that for a while and I think, this summer, I feel super happy and fulfilled by my life right now.

Rachelle: Yeah, me too. I feel, just like, in a specific way after last night and this weekend with you guys, it's just been like joy and bliss. Outside of this weekend, I feel like really everything is stable and happy and kind of good.

Ashley: But the world outside of us is so fucked. It's just my little life that feels secure.

Rachelle: I think that's part of it. The perspective of how fucked up the world is right now makes me appreciate my day to day, moment to moment life more.

Ashley: You don't know how long you'll be able to access joy and peace so you might as well get it.

WHAT CAN POETRY DO?

Rachelle: Everything.

Ashley: Nothing.

(laughter)

Rachelle: It can reorganise the way that a thought or feeling is articulated so you can understand it from a new point of view.

Ashley: I think it can transcend space and time, and heal. I find that when I can get something out onto paper, I can overcome it.

Rachelle: Yeah, or when I see it in someone else's work, something that I've been mulling over or am confused by, it sort of frees up that feeling for me.

WHAT CAN WE DO FOR POETRY?

Rachelle: I feel like when your interests give you joy, that can be a contagious thing. Other people can get into it in a new way. I think about my sister a lot. She's a scientist. She has very little interest in the arts apart from occasionally watching a movie or playing a video game or listening to music, but she would never read poetry if I wasn't sending her things every once in a while. And every time, she's like... blown away that she can have that experience and then she seeks it out more. I don't know.

I think if we love it and we make it a part of our lives, it will be something that other people in our lives have experiences with and maybe begin to love. And maybe then they go on and share it with other people.

YEATS FAMOUSLY SAID, YOU MUST CHOOSE BETWEEN THE LIFE AND THE WORK. DO YOU THINK THIS IS TRUE?

Ashley: Yeah, I think so.

Rachelle: I think I'm learning that it's true in a lot of ways. Or I think it's about time, where you spend your time. And if you don't spend your time thinking about the work and working towards the work, it will just always stay at a certain level or you won't be ready to access opportunities when they present themselves. I don't know. I think about it a lot in terms of wanting a family. As a woman, it's hard to imagine having time for the work and raising kids, sometimes. But I think that might just be... well it depends if you have help or a partner or... I don't know.

Ashley: Yeah, I think for me, I've always felt like my poetry is... how do I explain it? Oh my god, my brain is broken. I don't know. I feel like the work takes you away from life sometimes. There was a time in my life when it felt like they were one. But now I don't think they are.

Can you read the quote again?

YOU MUST CHOOSE BETWEEN THE LIFE AND THE WORK.

Ashley: Yeah, it's always about the balance, I guess. And I feel like I choose life more, these days.

Rachelle: I go through phases. Right now, I'm so much more focused on work because I can be. I'm like a full-time poet basically, right now, being in an MFA program. But when I get out of this program, I'm very scared to go back to a job and I don't know what to do with that yet. I want to just keep reading and writing all day. It's really been the best.

Lucy: I think that you can't make work if you don't have a life, obviously. I don't really agree with the quote, I guess. I don't think you have to choose one or the other. I mean, in terms of your art... Where else is it going to come from? You have to live.

Rachelle: I think you have to give yourself time to relax and go outside so that when you do write, you have things stored up but then you're also giving your brain a break from thinking about it. You can't think about anything constantly. You have to reset.

Lucy: Can I ask another question that just came to me?

Rachelle: Sure.

WHAT DO YOU THINK ABOUT THE ART OF CONVERSATION?

Ashley: I love talking to people. It's my favourite. It's a balance of receiving and giving in this living, breathing way that we communicate with one another. I love reading interviews with artists and listening to them. The art of engaging.

Lucy: Do you think of it as something that you're good at or that you work on or that you're conscious about?

Ashley: I feel like I'm a good communicator in that I ask people a lot of questions. You know when you have a conversation with someone and they don't ask you anything about yourself and take up all the space, I feel really confident in my ability to talk with people. But not if they're not interesting to me... though I find most people interesting.

Rachelle: I feel the same. I think I'm a good communicator. I don't know if I'm good at interviewing people in a literary setting or whatever, but I think in day-to-day conversations, I'm... fine.

(laughter)

Lucy: Is it something you think about? The quality of your conversations. The vocabulary you use. The sort of... ways you can divert or change the flow of what's happening. I didn't plan this question. I'm just curious. Something I've been thinking about. Do you feel like you go out of your way or want to have good conversations?

Rachelle: I think so. I think it is a really felt thing when you're hanging out with people and you're just not talking about anything interesting. It becomes really strained and almost anxious. I don't know if I'm thinking about it like that, but now I might be. About word choice and details.

Ashley: Yeah, I love talking with people but I also really like silence. And I think about psychic space a lot and how I'm always craving and carving out psychic space for myself where I can think my own thoughts and not have them be too influenced by other people. And yeah, I don't know. I guess I feel like I haven't been having enough conversations, lately, with people. I think that was a product of the pandemic, in a way, and I don't like talking on the phone. I'm very much a person of presence, so I wish I could talk with people more but I don't like talking on the phone. I find it irritating.

Lucy and Rachelle: Yeah.

Ashley: Do you guys like talking on the phone?

Lucy: Well, I never do it.

Rachelle: I do with my sister. She's the only person I can really talk to on the phone. I'll go for a walk and talk to her, or if I'm making dinner or something. I have to be doing something else. But otherwise, no, I'm no good at it. With other people.

I think what you said about psychic space is really important. I'm trying to get into the habit of not looking at my phone until a certain time of day. Especially with things like Twitter where everything is so abbreviated and negative and critical, which is not always a bad thing but I don't want to train my brain to think that way right out of bed. It feels really crowded in my head by noon. I'm also noticing that people, and I think it's because of the pandemic and because that's how we were connecting so much, it seems like when we're having conversations with people, it's like they have pre-formed things to say already. And they're all quippy. These little tweet-like things. Not as spontaneous or present or listening to one another. It just feels like saying things at each other, sometimes.

Lucy: Yeah, absolutely.

Rachelle: Have you noticed that?

Lucy: Especially when people first started to hang out again, it felt like every time I was in a group, it was really loud and everybody was just saying things and nobody was listening to anyone else.

Ashley: Yeah, because they were so excited to be in that space. It was weird. I totally agree. It's interesting that we all noticed that.

Rachelle: That first summer was brutal, in terms of... I would leave social situations and be like... Was that okay? Everyone seems fucked up!

Ashley: Exactly, that was it.

Rachelle: You go so long without having those social mirrors, where you can check yourself with people, that when you did it again, at least for me, I felt anxious. I wasn't sure how I was coming across, ever, because other people were coming across as bat-shit crazy to me.

(laughter)

Rachelle: So me too? I don't know.

Lucy: That thing you said about when people say, like... a line. I hate that.

Rachelle: It's like, I know you tweeted that or read it on Twitter two weeks ago, or something. I do it once in a while and I know, okay that didn't land because we're not on Twitter.

Lucy: It really is difficult to respond to when somebody does it. I just sort of look at them like, what are you doing?

Rachelle: It feels like a performance instead of a conversation where people are connecting. It feels like one person is performing and the other has to clap or laugh. It's annoying and dehumanising on a very subtle level.

Ashley: Yeah, I found that year so hard, and I don't like to say this because it's annoying, but I am an empath, and I can feel people's energy. So I kind of live in this world where conversation is one thing but then I pick up so much information without talking to people. I have this weird ability where I can tell, even if I'm walking by a stranger on the street, I can pick up what they're going through.

Rachelle: I experience a lot of hyper-vigilance stuff. I think because of certain experiences that have made me especially attuned to the energy of the room or a person's body language.

Ashley: I think women specifically need to do that. It's a way of keeping ourselves safe. You always have to be looking around.

Rachelle: And checking in to make sure people feel comfortable too.

Ashley: Who does that for us?

Rachelle: We do.

Lucy: We do.

Well, I guess we'd better stop because we all need to finish packing. Thank you so much for answering my questions when you're so hungover.

Rachelle: If this is going to be a thing that comes out, let them know that we're very hungover. We have not had coffee yet.

(laughter)

Rachelle: And I just took two allergy pills because we don't have any Advil, so I'm hoping that works.

(laughter)

Ashley: I actually still feel like I'm drunk.

Rachelle: Yeah me too!

WORK

I shaved my legs after class, standing up in the shower wearing a summer dress that makes me feel like I'm in southern Spain or Santorini. But I'm in Bed-Stuy.

Ça ça doit être ça va être chez la s

I'm using the speech-to-text function on my phone to write this, and it was set to the wrong language.

I texted with Sarah jubilantly about the job offer she has just received.

But then I walked over to Chris, who was sitting on the sofa, to receive a kiss on the nose and as I was pulling away I stubbed my toe on the glass table and it hurt a lot. I looked down to see blood on my toe and within an instant felt the familiar rush of pain. I shouted, 'It's taken a chunk!' which was overly dramatic and untrue but Chris gave me an ice cube and a paper towel and attached them to my foot with an elastic band and told me to raise my foot for elevation.

So now I've been stopped in my tracks.

I had been planning on going for a walk before meeting Sarah and other friends at the Commodore at 6:30pm for food and drinks and celebration.

We just went to the Commodore two nights ago, Sarah and I, so it's funny that we are going again.

I don't particularly like it there.

But Chris said recently that it's like our friends' version of *Central Perk*.

I am not so sure.

Although the nachos are unparalleled.

I walked three blocks to Herbert Von King Park and sat on the grass of the 'PASSIVE LAWN' doing my embroidery for a while before Francisca arrived to meet me. I'm doing an embroidery of a sunset from a few weeks ago in Conil de la Frontera.

I sewed tiny stitches of light into the sky and its reflection on the sand.

I looked up and identified some large graffiti across the park. It said, OMG THE DAY, the name of Theo's new chapbook.

Francisca showed up and offered me an apricot or a cigarette and I politely declined both.

I continued embroidering while we talked about the poetry reading we had both attended a few days ago, criticising the contents of the poems that were read and theorising about the changing role of identity in contemporary poetics, etc.

Elle va te elle va me faire des retours

It just did the French thing again.

Anyway, we also talked about the sort-of-relationship that she's been having with some guy and the last time I saw her she told me about how it had been going badly and, again, today, she updated me on how it's still going badly although there have been some magical moments in the interim. I listened for a while and then told her that I was almost 100% sure that this relationship would never work out and that I don't think she should expend so much energy on feeling heartbroken if she can help it. She laughed a lot when I said this and seemed to wish that somebody else had said it sooner.

I thought about people, well, boys that I haven't seen or spoken to for many years and how difficult it is to be a romantic person in your twenties.

Now I'm walking through Hasidic Williamsburg towards The Commodore and I will be early but I guess I can just hang out somewhere nearby before I'm supposed to meet everybody else.

As I walked, I listened to a podcast called Sentimental in the City, an episode about season six of the show, Sex and the City, which I was watching some of last night. There was one joke in the podcast which made me laugh out loud, almost in the faces of some young Hasidic women. It was a line that Samantha said after she saw a play starring her new boyfriend (Smith Jerrod), in which he got naked on stage, and later in bed she said to him, *'I've never been a fan of the theatre but get your cock out!'* which makes no sense and it made the podcast hosts laugh a lot, which in turn made me laugh a lot, on the street in Hasidic Williamsburg.

My little toe started to feel crushed on my right foot because of the band-aid assuaging my injury so I took one shoe off and put my toes under a fountain that some children were playing in as soon as I arrived at Domino park, overlooking the East River. Refreshing.

The park was full of wealthy young professionals doing yoga or drinking hard seltzers.

I noticed a girl writing in a notebook with an open novel beside her, so naturally I glanced down at the book as I passed by.

It was *On The Road* by Jack Kerouac, which made me smile and seemed unbelievable somehow.

How could somebody in Brooklyn be openly reading that book in this day and age?

I lay down on the patch of Astroturf under the Williamsburg Bridge and read for a while from the Rachel Cusk book, *A Life's Work*, which I bought a few days ago. It is a controversial memoir about being pregnant and having children, in which she doesn't seem to enjoy either of those things at all.

I'm doing research for the future.

I texted Chris and asked if he could bring my other shoes if he hadn't left yet and I also texted Sarah to ask if she was crossing the bridge I was sitting underneath and if she wanted to meet me on our way to the bar, which she did.

A short while later, Sarah came to meet me in the park and I wished her congratulations, in person, on getting a new job. We began to walk towards The Commodore, discussing various contemporary concerns including her new salary, which she described as 'mildly life-changing'.

We anticipated the rest of the summer.

On arrival at The Commodore, we met Jake who had secured a table for us outside on the street, but Sarah was dissatisfied with this location and so we decided to move to the inner terrace and Jake ordered a pitcher of beer for us to share. We talked about the so-called 'new right' and baseball and then Jordan arrived.

Jordan asked me what I was doing, on noticing me speaking into my phone about everything that has just happened, and I told him about the writing project I'm doing today (inspired by Brandon Brown's poetry book WORK) in which I have to write down everything that happens between finishing work one day and starting again the next.

Kristen arrived and everybody congratulated Sarah on her new job again.

Kristen and I went to the bar and she ordered tequila shots for everybody except me. I didn't want one. I ordered another pitcher of beer and some nachos for the table. The bartender was impatient.

Chris arrived. Everybody ate a lot of nachos, some people ordered additional food, and we talked for a long time about different things. Moby Dick. The so-called new right, again. Possible plans for later in the summer and 4th of July weekend when hopefully Sarah can have a week off work between jobs.

Another pitcher arrived.

I asked Jordan if he wanted to have children and he said he wasn't sure. He asked me if I did and I said I also didn't know. He asked me if Chris wanted to have children and I said not really, maybe sometimes.

We talked about various people we know and the challenges facing them. We discussed further possibilities for the 4th of July weekend.

I talked with Kristen about Sarah's new job. And about her own job at the same company. They are going to be working together.

I asked her to collaborate with me on something for my new book, Woman with Hat.

Around 10pm, we all decided to leave. I went to the bar to close my tab and a different bartender handed me a receipt for $20, when I had ordered around $38 worth of food and drinks. I signed it quickly and left.

Chris and I walked Kristen to the subway stop at Lorimer/Metropolitan.

Standing by the entrance to the train, they were both open to the idea of another drink, because the conversation didn't feel quite finished. But I said sorry, I don't have any energy left. I wanted to stay but I couldn't.

Chris and I decided to walk back to the apartment where we are staying. Kristen took the subway in the other direction.

On the walk back through Hasidic Williamsburg, I played Chris some audio from the podcast I listened to earlier about Sex and the City, specifically the part about the line by Samantha from the episode we watched yesterday.

When she said, *'I'm not usually a fan of the theatre but get your cock out!'* we both laughed a lot.

To see Chris laughing from a side angle as we glide through the Brooklyn night feels like some kind of returning.

We arrived back at the apartment and it smells very strongly of weed but nobody is here. My feet are very tired. I think I'll have a shower to rinse Brooklyn off of my body and then I will go to sleep soon. I feel very full of nachos and also like I haven't eaten real food since I arrived in America last week, but hopefully I can be healthier tomorrow.

I will wake up at 6:30am but it's okay. I only have...

No, actually, I have a lot of classes. Never mind.

Gabby messaged and asked if I still want to go to the Guggenheim tomorrow and I said yes and asked if we can go a little earlier because we had planned to go at 4pm but now I want to go at 3pm and she said that's fine so I booked my ticket and so did she and we will collaborate on something there for my new book, Woman with Hat.

I had a shower and brushed my teeth.

I went into the living room and Chris was lying flat on the sofa with a glass of wine balanced on his chest and I said 'Are you okay? You look tired' and he said, 'I'm just thinking about my book' and I said, 'Where is it?' and he said, 'That's what I'm thinking!'

Reading Rachel Cusk in bed until I fall asleep. 11:09pm.

11:20pm, I put the book down and re-confirm that my alarm is set for 6:30am.

Good night.

I dreamed about some kind of adventure game. Maté was there, and so was a man I used to work with who I don't like. He was following me. It was a bad feeling. I had to run around a village in somewhere like Greece, looking for clues. English people were there but I didn't know them. My body tensed up. It felt real and scary. I screamed at someone who had been told to follow me.

Woke up a few minutes before my alarm.

Raindrops on the window.

I am small spoon.

6:38am, I get up.

Delete 4 emails.

Brush my teeth.

I read an email from a student's parent that I have been nervous about and feel very happy.

I check my schedule and decide to shower during the thirty minute break between classes that I have from 8:30-9am.

Login to Zoom, 6:58am.

Computer propped up on a pillow on the sofa.

Virtual background in some clouds.

WOMAN WITH HAT 3

1. Now you've got to let me have the final word on this WOMAN WITH HAT business.

2. I had an idea, the other day, to have hats made with the words, WOMAN WITH HAT printed across the front of them.

3. Imagine yourself wearing one.

4. You would look amazing.

5. But what does WOMAN WITH HAT symbolise? What does it mean? What am I talking about? Why do I feel such a deep and sincere connection to the WOMAN WITH HAT phenomenon?

6. I'm not exactly a hat person myself.

7. Although very much a woman.

8. And honestly, I don't care what you think about this, but I love the work of Henri Matisse. I have embroidered many of his paintings. I remember when I went to the Fondation Louis Vuitton about five years ago when they were showing Shchukin's private collection and I was walking from room to room feeling neutral and then I entered into this part of the gallery that was wall to wall Matisse paintings, massive ones, and I was just absolutely

blown away. I was having a profound experience of art! I was completely in awe of the colours. Little me.

9. They were all post 1905, of course.

10. But what do any of these things have to do with one another?! Something about change?!

11. You can sense my frustration through my use of punctuation.

12. I want my friend to have the best life that it is possible for her to have!!!

13. I want for her to feel lifted up and loved and valuable and beautiful. I want her to be appreciated. I want her to be so powerful.

14. I want us to run through the streets of a city we've never been to before wearing hats that say WOMAN WITH HAT across the front of them.

15. I want us to be laughing.

EMBROIDERY IDEA

I had gotten in the habit, while I was by the sea, of swimming every day instead of running a lot. I was still going out about once a week, but it felt good to take the pressure off my knees for a while, to use some different muscles, and to swim across the bay every morning or afternoon or both. I felt strong.

When Liz came to visit, she said she'd like to go running, and so I took her out one morning.

I have a route when we're on Cape Cod, that involves circling around the small town nearby before heading out 'to the lighthouse,' as Virginia Woolf once titled a novel. About 7km in total. Liz told me that she had only recently gotten back into running after some time away and had been doing shorter distances. But I assured her that it was worth doing this particular route, to the lighthouse, and that we could just walk whenever, if we felt like it.

We ran for a while, and eventually reached the lighthouse, looked out at the water towards Martha's Vineyard. There is a memorial there for someone who died in one of the planes on 9/11. A young woman who had been married in the area shortly before she died. And I feel particularly struck by it every time I see it. Partly because I was also, as a young woman, married in this same area. And partly because of the *magnetic poetry* rendered in bronze across the centre of her memorial plaque.

Yes.

It's not the words themselves that interest me. A few short, pretty lines inspired by her wedding – actually I don't hate the poem, which of course I would expect to.

But rather, what fascinates me is the fact of the now very dated seeming *magnetic poetry* font, cast in metal, (each individual word separated from the others, as seen on your refrigerator during the early years of the twenty-first century) and set in stone, overlooking the bay towards Martha's Vineyard. Flowers growing around it all, unbothered by the flow of time.

I have thought about it often when I have been running up the hill towards the lighthouse and the lookout point. What would it feel like to die in an exploding aeroplane? How has the way we interpret 9/11 changed over the course of the past two decades? What would have been lost if they simply typed the *magnetic poetry* lines in the same font as the rest of the memorial? At what point did everyone, collectively as a culture, remove the *magnetic poetry* kits from their refrigerator doors? Is *magnetic poetry* recyclable?

None of this is what I'm really here to write about. But these are some of the subjects I raised with Liz on our run that morning before we set out on the return leg of our journey.

I also told her about how I had been running with Mahshid that time and how I had tried to distract her by telling a story. As we started running up and down hills, and the morning sun started to burn, she said that I could do the same thing for her.

RUNNING STORY NUMBER TWO

I wonder what you think of this. The idea of me running around with some friend of mine who's too tired to speak out loud, telling them stories about my life. It seems a little self-indulgent to write about. Although what doesn't?

I want to write down these two stories about running. And they make the most sense to me within their original context.

More running.

(As an aside, I went to the Musée d'Orsay last week with Gabby. It is mid-August as I write this and Paris is completely empty except for the tourist sites. We waited in line for a long time in extreme heat, and then once we were allowed inside, were met by throngs of indifferent tourists zigzagging their way from room to room in vague search of famous paintings by Van Gogh. I lost Gabby and wandered through the upstairs galleries of well-known impressionist paintings, manoeuvring my way through thick crowds of sweating people and quickly decided to go off-piste within the museum. I would need to find something to look at that nobody else cares about.

In an empty room of art nouveau furniture, lamenting the fourteen euros I had paid to step inside of the overheated former train station, I decided that I would simply curate my own experience and think about writing this book instead of anything else. I listened to Kylie Minogue, drifted from room to room. And somewhere, surrounded by Roman statues, had the idea for these stories.)

So, the story that I wanted to tell Liz was about last Christmas. 2021.

The first COVID Christmas in 2020 had been an emotional disaster for us. Navigating the French government's everchanging rules and restrictions, in conjunction with their wildly contrasting interpretations by different branches and generations of extended family proved to be a challenge that nobody was equipped to deal with. Morally charged ideas about what was and wasn't appropriate or safe, mixed with an inherent seasonal pressure for people to come together and celebrate made for the kind of stressful situations and dynamics that I can only assume you also waded through during the hardest months of the pandemic. So I won't go into detail.

But will we ever be able to recover from that time?

Will our relationships to one another ever go back to how they were before?

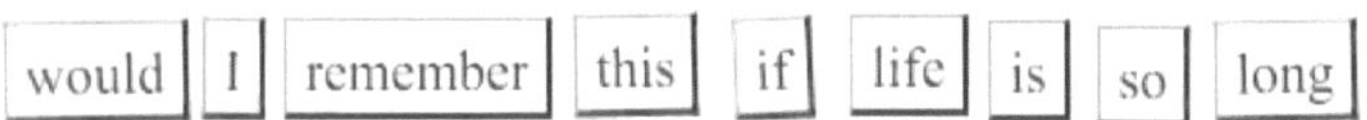

Regardless of the long-term consequences, when the next Christmas came around, I was desperate to go home.

By late 2021, we no longer had such intense restrictions in France. We were double and then soon triple-vaccinated. I had been able to travel home to visit my family in England at the end of the summer. We confidently booked our flights for Christmas.

But come mid-December, the Omicron variant had emerged, and of course, the French government wanted to limit its spread.

Cases were soaring out of control in the UK, and diplomatic relations over the past few years have been increasingly fraught, so France decided to close the border. Again.

This was the 16th of December.

They said it was effective as of tomorrow.

Our flight was booked for the 19th.

I was on a break between classes, had been wrapping presents, the news was streaming from my computer. I started texting my parents, started texting Chris. He was already in Paris. I tried calling the airline. No answer. I looked online, and it would cost me several hundred euros to change the tickets to one of the last flights leaving from France tomorrow. But I decided I had to do it.

I took the train to Paris later that evening. We were supposed to be meeting some friends visiting from New York over the weekend. Now they would arrive the same day we had to leave. But going home felt more important.

The next morning, we decided to take the RER to the airport. Charles de Gaulle. There was a train strike, but limited services were still supposed to be running, and I had spent so much money on changing the tickets, I didn't feel like I could afford to spend fifty euros more on a taxi.

We left with plenty of hours to spare and got on the Métro towards Gare du Nord, where we would change to the RER. But the Métro got stuck somewhere underground. It was completely packed full of people. A suspicious bag had been left somewhere and all the trains were stopped. We stood together pressed against the crowds for a long time and sweated into our coats.

But we still had time.

Eventually we pulled into Gare du Nord and ran up the steps with all of our stuff. An announcement: The RERs were no longer running. Or maybe the next one was in an hour. It wasn't clear. There were hundreds of people on the platform waiting for it.

We would have to get a taxi after all, we conceded.

We ran out of the train station and flagged down a taxi, told him we were going to the airport. Said goodbye to fifty euros on top of the twenty we had already paid for the train.

As we headed towards the Peripherique to get onto the highway, the traffic was at a standstill. I sat in the back of the car, putting the directions into Google maps, and time was getting tighter.

The taxi driver told us it would clear up as soon as we got out of the city, but then it didn't. Something had happened. An accident on the Peripherique.

I started to cry.

I had spent hundreds of euros on changing our tickets to the last possible flight before the border closed, and now we were going to miss the plane. And for the second year in a row, I was going to miss Christmas with my family.

I don't even care about Christmas!

But I felt like I needed something.

To go home.

To feel normal.

To stop feeling angry!

As we inched forwards on the Peripherique, I was absolutely sobbing in the back of the car, uncontrollably crying. I texted my mum and my sister and told them that we had messed everything up and that maybe we weren't going to make it.

I had been working so hard for the past few weeks, doing extra hours to pay for presents, and I haven't even mentioned this part yet, but I was about to lose my job of four years, didn't know how I was going to earn a living after the next month. And yet here I was throwing money away.

As the minutes went by, it became more and more impossible.

The taxi driver was kind. He told me to try not to worry. He said, *it's only money*. I said thank you.

But it wasn't.

We inched along the highway and I FaceTimed my mum crying and told her that we were only going to make it to the airport after check-in had closed.

She said it wasn't my fault, that I had done this journey many times before and it had always been okay in the past. I couldn't predict that all these things would go wrong.

I felt like a failure!

Like this is why you're supposed to be rich. So you can afford a fifty-euro taxi to the airport and never feel this stressed.

Chris was just staring out of the window on the other side of the car.

I started thinking about how we were even going to get back to Paris from the airport, seeing as there were no trains.

We would have to pay even more money.

My mum looked online and told me the flight was due to leave from terminal 2E. She said whenever you get there, just try, just run out of the taxi.

I looked at all the information I had from the airline and they were telling me to go to terminal 2A.

Check-in closed and we were still a few miles away.

When we eventually arrived at the airport, it was about 20 minutes before the flight was due to leave. It was not going to happen. We thanked the driver and apologised for the scene I'd made.

We had asked him to take us to terminal 2A because that's what the airline told us, but when we ran into the terminal, it turned out that my mum was right. They had changed our terminal without even telling us.

I couldn't breathe.

Chris asked someone working at the airport how to get to terminal 2E and he pointed ahead of us and said it was about a twenty minute walk that way.

I honestly don't know why but in that moment my body just decided that I wasn't giving up and I started running. I was wearing a coat and a hat and I was pulling a suitcase and I just started running through Charles de Gaulle airport. I knew it wasn't possible. But I had to get as close as I could.

We ran, Chris a few steps behind me and thinking I was completely insane, along long corridors connecting terminals, through the train station, out into another terminal, onto the next one. I just put my phone in my pocket and stopped looking at the time. After several minutes and over a kilometre, we arrived at terminal 2E.

I didn't think that I'd be able to get into the security area seeing as our check-in had already closed, but when I scanned my boarding pass, it let me in. We ran down into the passport control area and told someone we were late. They pushed us to the front.

Then we ran through into the bag check area and for the first time ever, there was nobody there. We took off our shoes and coats and pulled out our laptops and liquids and had our full bodies scanned. Scrambled to put everything back into our bags and kept on running.

We ran up the stairs and through duty free and looked at the gate number. It was five minutes until the flight was due to leave, and we still had a long way to go, they were never going to let us on the plane. We ran the length of terminal 2E, checking off the gate numbers as we passed them, and as we got closer a woman wearing the airline's uniform was walking towards us with a clipboard. She said the name of our destination out loud with a question mark and I said YES! She said, *you can do it! Keep running!*

So I kept running toward the gate and a minute later arrived there, out of breath and covered in tears, and waited for a couple of seconds for Chris to catch up. The girls who were managing the check-in desk had Yorkshire accents and said, *'Don't worry, we wouldn't leave without you!'*

They checked our passports and smiled and apologised for the change in terminal. We walked onto the plane and sat down. Completely dehydrated and emotional. I pulled out my phone and texted my mum a photo from inside the plane.

She texted a laughing emoji and said HOW?! And then said she was crying.

We arrived home on one of the last flights allowed into the country before the border closed, before Christmas.

This is what I train for!

WHO NARRATES HISTORY?

Big animals that can eat you
Housesit owners
Walt Whitman telling a reporter he fucked Oscar Wilde
Italian men from 600 years ago

I went to Liz and Will's apartment for dinner. It was late July and a heatwave. Chris came early and ate with us but then he had to leave and go to another friend's place for drinks. The remaining three of us went up on the roof and stood around as the sun set and talked about Emily Dickinson and Oscar Wilde and Virginia Wolfe. We talked about how much it helps to know the story of an artist's life in order to understand and appreciate their work. We took a lot of photos of one another against the peach-orange sky. It felt kind of perfect.

Earlier that day I had been at The Met by myself and picked up two conversation-starter cards from outside of an exhibition I didn't look at.

One said,

What is representation?

Which, I'm not sure.

The other said,

Who narrates history?

I put them on the table before the meal was served and we discussed the questions as we ate.

Linguine, goat cheese salad, and then later, raspberries and cheesecake.

Many topics were covered.

As ever, with Liz and Will, the conversation was exuberant.

Sometimes, throughout the evening, Liz got up from the sofa and noted things on one of the cards.

We drank all the wine and the dog rested.

As I left their apartment, early enough for an early morning the next morning, I noticed what she had written and read her notes, smiling. Took a photo.

Wrote this on the subway the next day when I saw the photo on my phone.

Who narrates history? We had wondered.

When all along...

We do!

MOUNTAINS

This time I was almost sure of it. It made total sense. We had done it when I was ovulating. He hadn't pulled out fast enough, but I didn't really care. It felt like something that would happen eventually. And then soon enough, my body started to feel differently. The blood did not come. I was trying not to fall asleep at three o'clock every afternoon. I had felt nauseous on four separate occasions.

I waited until five days late and ordered a test from Amazon. It arrived two days later on the seventh afternoon.

It was during the time that the test was in transit that I guess I let my mind wander. I started figuring out how 'far along' I could be, and when, therefore, the baby would arrive. I imagined myself six months pregnant at Christmas, too embarrassed to be seen by my family.

I accepted that we would have to move to Paris. Maybe I could go to the American Hospital and do the whole process in English. Or maybe this would be the push I needed to finally force myself to perfect my French. I could lie flat like a whale-pig and practice the subjunctive.

I imagined telling my friends the news. Not in a way that felt like a celebration, but rather with a tone of resignation.

I regret to inform you that it's the end of an era. Feel free to abandon me now.

But really, who was I going to talk to? There is nobody I'd feel comfortable with. I hadn't been empathetic enough towards my one friend who actually has a baby while she was pregnant. How could I have been? I didn't know what it was like then. I imagined texting her out of the blue, politely expressing interest in her life, and then feeling too stupid to tell her the news.

I suppose this is why all the healthcare websites recommend antenatal classes and forming bonds with fellow pregnant women in your local community. But I can only imagine such people would be total lunatics.

Although I suppose they could also help me with my French.

But seriously, the worst part is how calmly I felt about the whole situation. It just seemed like, okay, so this is my new life plan. I need to incubate a tiny human inside my body until next February and then care for them indefinitely. Basically, until I die.

I thought about traveling to Muslim countries in the meantime, seeing as I wouldn't be drinking anyway.

Imagined moving out of our apartment, and decorating a new place absolutely drenched with natural light. Walking the streets of Paris in the wintertime with a full belly under my coat and feeling the eyes of men upon me.

I wanted the baby to be born in France, although I also wanted them to have the three passports they'd be entitled to, in case of future geopolitical conflicts. I imagined a spoiled, bilingual brat. And that was another reason why I would need to perfect my French before they were born. I couldn't have them undermining me or mocking my accent.

I would need to work really hard on sounding Parisian so that I could contend with their teachers when we'd have petty disputes over handwriting exercises in six years time.

By then I would be forty years old and still beautiful, although the teacher would be twenty-seven and fresh faced, probably from the mountains. I guess that's fine.

Which third language would we teach the child? I'm tempted to say Chinese, but maybe it would be Arabic.

They would probably have a thing about how they *have* been to Saudi Arabia but they don't remember because they were still inside mummy's tummy.

I hope they wouldn't act snootily towards their grandparents or cousins.

I hope they would be able to run fast and paint well and sing beautifully.

I would feel uncomfortable if they couldn't sing.

I'm so nervous opening the test packet. I am almost certain the results will be positive. I go into the bathroom and pee into a cup and then dip the test into it. Replace the cap and lay it flat.

A single horizontal line appears. I stare at it. Nothing else happens.

He shouts to me from outside the bathroom. 'Are you waiting for the results in there?'

I open the door and tell him, 'It says negative.'

'Really?'

I bring the test out and place it on the kitchen counter.

The whole future disappears.

It's weird.

I still don't understand.

If I'm not pregnant, then what *is* wrong with me?

TEACHER

I was sitting in Washington Square Park, one hot July morning, with my thirteen-year-old student, both drawing in our notebooks, when some women wearing matching pale pink t-shirts arrived by the fountain and started yelling into a megaphone, like, *Good Morning New York City!*

I sighed to myself a little, like, *Here we go...*

Then they started to shout about how people in some states no longer have legal access to safe abortions and told stories about women who have had to travel long distances and pay lots of money to terminate their unwanted pregnancies, just in the past few weeks, since Roe vs Wade was overturned by the Supreme Court.

People around us, who had until then mostly been minding their own business, immediately started clapping for them and yelling supportive slogans.

A middle-aged white man, sitting on the edge of the fountain, who was particularly vocal, started chanting, *your body, your choice, your body, your choice.* And other men around the park joined in.

I smiled at the men weakly and continued drawing.

But one by one, each woman in the pale pink t-shirt group would take her turn with the megaphone and share her own specific message. And I quickly began to feel moved by the fact of them doing this. Taking time out of their lives to yell in the park about something that makes most of us feel so powerless.

My student was drawing an anime-style face in her notebook and hadn't reacted at all so I asked her if she understood what they were saying.

She is not a native English speaker but she is basically fluent so I assumed that she was following their dispatches, but she said that she had no idea what they were talking about.

I realised it was more a matter of context.

Other questions I had already tried to answer during our three days together in New York:

1. Aren't those men too hot? (We had walked on the edge of Hasidic Williamsburg briefly.)
2. Why did people want to fly planes into those buildings anyway? (We had passed by the 9/11 memorial fountains.)

I told her that the pale pink t-shirt women were protesting restrictions on abortion rights and asked her if she knew what this word means, *abortion*.

She said no.

So I told her that sometimes people can be pregnant when they don't want to be and that abortion is the medical procedure used to stop this.

I told her that the verb *abort* means to end something before it's finished.

I told her that in Europe, where we both live, women have had access to safe abortions for a very long time.

I told her that if either of us ever needs one, we can go to the doctor and they can do this for us, for free.

I told her, this is our right.

But then I told her that recently in America, in many places in the country, access has been restricted to this kind of medical treatment and that this is very, very bad for women.

In fact, it is very bad for everyone.

People will be forced to give birth to babies that they don't want to and/or cannot take care of.

She didn't look up while I was telling her this.

She just nodded and continued drawing.

In the background one of the women was doing a call and response with the crowd, *my uterus my choice, my uterus my choice...*

I told her that it was very cool and brave that these women were doing this.

And I noticed, as I was speaking, that it was very difficult to get these words out of my mouth without sounding like my voice was breaking. That I had to speak very slowly. That I was relieved to be wearing sunglasses.

THE SUMMER CAMP ADDRESS

Hi everyone.

Welcome to summer camp!

Thank you to everybody for travelling here!

And thank you for hosting us!

It's really great to see you all and to be here.

Probably by now you have all been introduced to each other, if you didn't already know each other for years prior, but I thought we could try something to help the people who don't know each other well to get to know each other.

So basically, we'll go around the group and each person can introduce someone else to us all, by telling us a brief memory or fact about them.

Rachelle introduced Bookin, mentioning that he lives in Buffalo and co-founded Peach Mag.

Bookin introduced Chris, mentioning that he wrote Teen Surf Goth.

Chris introduced Kristen, mentioning that she edits The Bushwick Review.

Kristen introduced Francisca, mentioning that she saw her read at my book launch last year.

Francisca introduced me, mentioning that we met in Lisbon.

I introduced Aidan, mentioning an inside joke from Liz's wedding.

Aidan introduced Caroline, mentioning the first time that he met her in Northampton.

Caroline introduced Emma, mentioning that they saw Waxahatchee together last year.

Okay nice, so hopefully that covers everyone.

So I was thinking about what I'd like to talk to everyone about, as part of the literary programming for this evening, and one thing that I've been thinking about sometimes in the past few months is that this year marks ten years since I started the online art and literature magazine, Shabby Doll House, which is the project through which I met basically all of you and perhaps some of you also met each other.

So obviously, that's very cool, and kind of amazing. When I think about all of the things that I personally, and we collectively have written, published, made, etc, over the past few years, I think, wow nice... Life has been a great success!

But life, if we're lucky, is very long. And ten years is nothing in the grand history of art and literature. So perhaps we don't need to make such a big deal out of that.

Though on the other hand, of course we have all known many people throughout these past years who have written things we have admired, been inspired or moved by, and then that person has disappeared off the face of the earth, and, to put it politely, found space in their life for other things, instead of writing, or art, or publishing magazines, or attending summer camps. Which makes total sense. Life is expensive and writing is almost always a waste of money.

Also, I know that many of you have perhaps had the experience of writing and publishing a book, feeling that it is the start of something exciting. A new phase in your life as an artistic person. Only to find the aftermath underwhelming, the reception of the work subdued, the work of pushing it to readers arduous. And even when something is received with heaps of praise, you don't hear any of it, don't accept it or take it on board. Forget it quickly. The achievement you've been working towards for years was completely meaningless and you feel worse than you ever did before.

Just kidding, it's not that bad.

But anyway, as we all know, none of that stuff was what compelled you to write a book in the first place.

You wrote because you had to.

Not to be dramatic.

But there's no way you would find yourself here at this summer camp if you hadn't felt compelled to share something of your experience on this earth through the medium of language.

You felt that long before you knew any of the people here.

And you will continue to feel it long after the rest of us are all dead...

I want to talk to you tonight about finishing your second books.

And ask you, in the words of Gwen Stefani, '*What you waiting, what you waiting, what you waiting, what you waiting, what you waiting, what you waiting for?*'

Prestige doesn't matter.

Publishing on big presses doesn't matter.

Publishing on small presses doesn't even matter.

Honestly, nothing really matters.

So how do we continue?

How do we keep on going?

We will only be able to do it together!

So tonight I would like to ask all of you, how are you feeling creatively at this time in your life? Have you been working on anything in particular? Or thinking about some kind of idea or theme? Are you sitting on a project that nobody knows about? Are you feeling hopeless or disconnected from your work? Are you thriving artistically?

I suppose I'd like to ask everybody to try not to give excuses in their answers, but you know, if you have a good one, feel free to include it.

Let's go around the circle and share with each other, so we know where we're all at right now. Perhaps we can talk to each other about all of this throughout the weekend.

I opened the discussion by describing this project, WOMAN WITH HAT. I said I didn't have a big idea for a next book yet, but I wanted to write for fun anyway, and I thought that doing so would push me forwards towards new ideas.

And then, one by one, each person went around the circle and explained their current situation. Everybody took it seriously and answered in earnest. Some people were thriving, others feeling lost. If you're reading this in the future, maybe take a minute to answer the question for yourself...

To close, I'd like to encourage everybody to publish their second book. Or third book. Or whatever it is you've been working on.

Your work may be met with resistance, your work may be ignored, but only by putting it out into the world, will you be able to make progress for yourself. And I mean that!

Okay, thank you for listening.

Have a nice weekend.

LADY WINDERMERE'S FAN CLUB

THE PERSONS OF THE PLAY

LUCY
GABBY
CHRIS
JORDAN
BROOKE
SARAH JEAN

THE SCENES OF THE PLAY

ACT 1. THE PORCH BY NIGHT
ACT 2. THE LIVING ROOM IN THE EARLY HOURS OF THE MORNING
ACT 3. THE PORCH AT LUNCH TIME

The action of the play takes place within twenty-four hours, beginning on a Friday evening at 11:30pm, and ending the next day around 3pm.

On the porch of an old house on Cape Cod. It's 11:30pm and Jordan, Brooke and Sarah Jean have just arrived from New York. The atmosphere is convivial. Everybody is seated around the dinner table having just eaten an elaborate feast prepared by Chris. It has taken the guests around six hours to drive up to the house and after dinner, they are tired. As they digest, Lucy and Gabby get up from the table and whisper to one another excitedly. Momentarily, they stand together in the centre of the porch with an offer.

LUCY: Would you like for me and Gabby to perform a scene from *(holding up a copy of the book) Lady Windermere's Fan* by Oscar Wilde?

(nervous silence)

SARAH JEAN: *(leaning back and reaching for a weed vape)* Okay!

Gabby and Lucy take their positions on two garden chairs separated by a small metal table. The porch light is directly above them. The rest of the group look alternately nervous and stoic. They refill their glasses from a box of red wine that Chris brings out to the table.

LUCY: I bought this book earlier today at the library sale for $1 and this afternoon, I asked Gabby if she wanted to read some of it with me, and we ended up doing the whole first act together and laughing a lot. So I thought we could perform a short scene for you while you relax after dinner.

(Turning to Gabby, showing her a particular page of the book and whispering)

So we'll just go as far as this part?

GABBY: Okay cool. Wait one second, I need to open the PDF on my phone.

LUCY: Oh yeah, if anyone wants to follow along with the script, I'm sending the link to the group chat now. We're starting at the beginning of the first act so you don't need any context. Chris, do you want to play Parker?

CHRIS: *(Shaking his head and smiling as he opens the link)* Okay sure. *(Turning to the rest of the group)* Parker is the butler.

GABBY: *(Using a grandiose, old-fashioned English accent with which it takes her twice as long to say each word than you would usually expect)* I'm Lord Darlington!

LUCY: *(Speaking in a clipped, Queen Elizabeth II style accent)* And I'm Lady Windermere.

Jordan, Brooke and Sarah Jean exchange bemused glances with one another.

SCENE

Morning-room of Lord Windermere's house in Carlton House Terrace.

[Lady Windermere/Lucy *is at table R., arranging roses in a blue bowl.*]

[*Enter* Parker/Chris.]

Parker/Chris. Is your ladyship at home this afternoon?

Lady Windermere/Lucy. Yes—who has called?

Parker/Chris. Lord Darlington, my lady.

Lady Windermere/Lucy. [*Hesitates for a moment.*] Show him up—and I'm at home to any one who calls.

Parker/Chris. Yes, my lady.

[*Exit C.*]

Lady Windermere/Lucy. It's best for me to see him before to-night. I'm glad he's come.

[*Enter* Parker/Chris *C.*]

Parker/Chris. Lord Darlington,

[*Enter* Lord Darlington *C.*]

[*Exit* Parker.]

Lord Darlington/Gabby. How do you do, Lady Windermere?

Lady Windermere/Lucy. How do you do, Lord Darlington? No, I can't shake hands with you. My hands are all wet with these roses. Aren't they lovely? They came up from Selby this morning.

Lord Darlington/Gabby. They are quite perfect. [*Sees a fan lying on the table.*] And what a wonderful fan! May I look at it?

Lady Windermere/Lucy. Do. Pretty, isn't it! It's got my name on it, and everything. I have only just seen it myself. It's my husband's birthday present to me. You know to-day is my birthday?

Lord Darlington/Gabby. No? Is it really?

Lady Windermere/Lucy. Yes, I'm of age to-day. Quite an important day in my life, isn't it? That is why I am giving this party to-night. Do sit down. [*Still arranging flowers.*]

Lord Darlington/Gabby. [*Sitting down.*] I wish I had known it was your birthday, Lady Windermere. I would have covered the whole street in front of your house with flowers for you to walk on. They are made for you.

[*A short pause.*]

Lady Windermere/Lucy. Lord Darlington, you annoyed me last night at the Foreign Office. I am afraid you are going to annoy me again.

Lord Darlington/Gabby. I, Lady Windermere?

[*Enter* Parker/Chris *and* Footman *C., with tray and tea things.*]

Lady Windermere/Lucy. Put it there, Parker. That will do. [*Wipes her hands with her pocket-handkerchief, goes to tea-table, and sits down.*] Won't you come over, Lord Darlington?

[*Exit* Parker *C.*]

Lord Darlington/Gabby. [*Takes chair and goes across L.C.*] I am quite miserable, Lady Windermere. You must tell me what I did. [*Sits down at table L.*]

Lady Windermere/Lucy. Well, you kept paying me elaborate compliments the whole evening.

Lord Darlington/Gabby. [*Smiling.*] Ah, nowadays we are all of us so hard up, that the only pleasant things to pay *are* compliments. They're the only things we *can* pay.

Lady Windermere/Lucy. [*Shaking her head.*] No, I am talking very seriously. You mustn't laugh, I am quite serious. I don't like compliments, and I don't see why a man should think he is pleasing a woman enormously when he says to her a whole heap of things that he doesn't mean.

Lord Darlington/Gabby. Ah, but I did mean them. [*Takes tea which she offers him.*]

Lady Windermere/Lucy. [*Gravely.*] I hope not. I should be sorry to have to quarrel with you, Lord Darlington. I like you very much, you know that. But I shouldn't like you at all if I thought you were what most other men are. Believe me, you are better than most other men, and I sometimes think you pretend to be worse.

Lord Darlington/Gabby. We all have our little vanities, Lady Windermere.

Lady Windermere/Lucy. Why do you make that your special one? [*Still seated at table L.*]

Lord Darlington/Gabby. [*Still seated L.C.*] Oh, nowadays so many conceited people go about Society pretending to be good, that I think it shows rather a sweet and modest disposition to pretend to be bad. Besides, there is this to be said. If you pretend to be good, the world takes you very seriously. If you pretend to be bad, it doesn't. Such is the astounding stupidity of optimism.

Lady Windermere/Lucy. Don't you *want* the world to take you seriously then, Lord Darlington?

Lord Darlington/Gabby. No, not the world. Who are the people the world takes seriously? All the dull people one can think of, from the Bishops down to the bores. I should like *you* to take me very seriously, Lady Windermere, *you* more than any one else in life.

Lady Windermere/Lucy. Why—why me?

Lord Darlington/Gabby. [*After a slight hesitation.*] Because I think we might be great friends. Let us be great friends. You may want a friend some day.

Lady Windermere/Lucy. Why do you say that?

Lord Darlington/Gabby. Oh!—we all want friends at times.

Lady Windermere/Lucy. I think we're very good friends already, Lord Darlington. We can always remain so as long as you don't–

Lord Darlington/Gabby. Don't what?

Lady Windermere/Lucy. Don't spoil it by saying extravagant silly things to me. You think I am a Puritan, I suppose? Well, I have something of the Puritan in me. I was brought up like that. I am glad of it. My mother died when I was a mere child. I lived always with Lady Julia, my father's elder sister, you know. She was stern to me, but she taught me what the world is forgetting, the difference that there is between what is right and what is wrong. *She* allowed of no compromise. *I* allow of none.

Lord Darlington/Gabby. My dear Lady Windermere!

Lady Windermere/Lucy. [*Leaning back on the sofa.*] You look on me as being behind the age.–Well, I am! I should be sorry to be on the same level as an age like this.

Lord Darlington/Gabby. You think the age very bad?

Lady Windermere/Lucy. Yes. Nowadays people seem to look on life as a speculation. It is not a speculation. It is a sacrament. Its ideal is Love. Its purification is sacrifice.

Lord Darlington/Gabby. [*Smiling.*] Oh, anything is better than being sacrificed!

Lady Windermere/Lucy. [*Leaning forward.*] Don't say that.

Lord Darlington/Gabby. I do say it. I feel it–I know it.

[*Enter* Parker *C.*]

Parker/Chris. The men want to know if they are to put the carpets on the terrace for to-night, my lady?

Lady Windermere/Lucy. You don't think it will rain, Lord Darlington, do you?

Lord Darlington/Gabby. I won't hear of its raining on your birthday!

Lady Windermere/Lucy. Tell them to do it at once, Parker.

[*Exit* Parker *C.*]

Jordan, Brooke and Sarah Jean observe the performance with gradually increasing interest and one by one, open the link to the script to follow along. Each person in the group expresses surprise at the clarity of the dialogue, and the precision of the humour, having not thought of Oscar Wilde for a long time, if ever.

Lord Darlington/Gabby. [*Still seated.*] Do you think then—of course I am only putting an imaginary instance—do you think that in the case of a young married couple, say about two years married, if the husband suddenly becomes the intimate friend of a woman of—well, more than doubtful character—is always calling upon her, lunching with her, and probably paying her bills—do you think that the wife should not console herself?

Lady Windermere/Lucy. [*Frowning.*] Console herself?

Lord Darlington/Gabby. Yes, I think she should—I think she has the right.

Lady Windermere/Lucy. Because the husband is vile—should the wife be vile also?

Lord Darlington/Gabby. Vileness is a terrible word, Lady Windermere.

Lady Windermere/Lucy. It is a terrible thing, Lord Darlington.

Lord Darlington/Gabby. Do you know I am afraid that good people do a great deal of harm in this world. Certainly the greatest harm they do is that they make badness of such extraordinary importance. It is absurd to divide people into good and bad. People are either charming or tedious. I take the side of the charming, and you, Lady Windermere, can't help belonging to them.

Lady Windermere/Lucy. Now, Lord Darlington. [*Rising and crossing R., front of him.*] Don't stir, I am merely going to finish my flowers. [*Goes to table R.C.*]

Lord Darlington/Gabby. [*Rising and moving chair.*] And I must say I think you are very hard on modern life, Lady Windermere. Of course there is much against it, I admit. Most women, for instance, nowadays, are rather mercenary.

Lady Windermere/Lucy. Don't talk about such people.

Lord Darlington/Gabby. Well then, setting aside mercenary people, who, of course, are dreadful, do you think seriously that women who have committed what the world calls a fault should never be forgiven?

Lady Windermere/Lucy. [*Standing at table.*] I think they should never be forgiven.

Lord Darlington/Gabby. And men? Do you think that there should be the same laws for men as there are for women?

Lady Windermere/Lucy. Certainly!

Lord Darlington/Gabby. I think life too complex a thing to be settled by these hard and fast rules.

Lady Windermere/Lucy. If we had 'these hard and fast rules,' we should find life much more simple.

Lord Darlington/Gabby. You allow of no exceptions?

Lady Windermere/Lucy. None!

Lord Darlington/Gabby. Ah, what a fascinating Puritan you are, Lady Windermere!

Lady Windermere/Lucy. The adjective was unnecessary, Lord Darlington.

Lord Darlington/Gabby. I couldn't help it. I can resist everything except temptation.

Lady Windermere/Lucy. You have the modern affectation of weakness.

Lord Darlington/Gabby. [*Looking at her.*] It's only an affectation, Lady Windermere.

[*Enter* Parker/Chris *C.*]

Parker/Chris. The Duchess of Berwick and Lady Agatha Carlisle.

[*Enter the* Duchess of Berwick and Lady Agatha Carlisle *C.*]

LUCY: Oh, we have some new characters... Does anybody want to... take on a role?

JORDAN: Okay!

LUCY: Nice! Okay, you can be The Duchess of Berwick...

Jordan, Brooke and Chris take on new roles as more characters are introduced. There is an Australian character named Mr Hopper, so naturally Jordan embodies this role too. Brooke, who at first appears uncomfortable with acting, takes on the role of Lord Augustus, and finds her feet delivering his trademark vocabulary. Demmed vocabulary. Chris takes on the role of Lord Windermere when he enters the scene. Sarah Jean sits quietly, laughing and taking photos, following along with the script on her phone and providing a generous audience. The group perform the entire first act of Lady Windermere's Fan as an ensemble on the porch, surrounded by dinner plates and filling their glasses often with more wine from the box.

When the first act is over it is close to 1am and the group have been loudly acting out their roles on the porch in a quiet, almost silent residential area, so together they concede that they should move into the house, where they resume their performance in the living room.

As act two brings further drama, and the plot, as they say, thickens, the group become truly engrossed in the production. At one point, during a decisive conversation between Lady Windermere (Lucy) and Lord Darlington (Gabby), the actors both rise to their feet to breathlessly deliver the scene standing in front of the fireplace. Sarah Jean and Jordan, on the sofa, begin scrolling quickly through their scripts to find out if the scene will be resolved with a kiss.

Later, Jordan delivers a scene in which he is playing multiple characters with a kaleidoscope of accents all in conversation with one another. His interpretation of Mrs Erlynne, in particular, has the whole party in hysterics as they struggle to compose themselves sufficiently to deliver their own lines.

Something happens to the group.

They actually lose themselves in the literature and experience a kind of fun they never have before, connecting with this language from the past, and in some surprising way, with one another. By the time they finish the second act, at close to 3 o'clock in the morning, they have all expressed themselves in a manner they couldn't have predicted, delivered voices they didn't know they were capable of, and laughed so much they lost any sense of self-consciousness. In part because the situation is preposterous. Who does stuff like this? And in part because the play itself is just so funny.

Lucy (Lady Windermere) takes out her phone in the midst of the production and records an audio file from the last eleven minutes of the second act, which is how she can be so sure it really happened.

The play is completed, a little hungover, with lunch the following day.[2]

[2] Like all of Oscar Wilde's work, *Lady Windermere's Fan* is in the public domain. I highly recommend reading the rest of the play. It's wonderful.

WOMAN WITH HAT 4

1. We arrived in Budapest around noon, took a bus to the centre and hung out in a cafe for a while as we waited for our Airbnb to become available at 2pm. Pulled our suitcases along cobbled streets for five minutes, followed the instructions in the email, entered the code, and an old woman greeted us in Hungarian and showed us to our place.

We smiled and nodded at everything she said, understanding none of the specifics, but recognising that it all seemed ultimately unimportant.

We showered, unpacked a little, tested the Wi-Fi and got ready to go out. Neither of us had to work that day. Travel day.

I stood by the door waiting for Chris and caught up on the group chat with his family. His dad was in New York. His brother was in Paris. And his mom had said something about how things were not looking good for the Queen.

I opened BBC news on my phone and scrolled through the live updates which said that she was under medical supervision at Balmoral and that all of her various family members were on their way there.

We walked out of the Airbnb and headed towards a vegan falafel place which I had found online a couple of weeks earlier. On the way, we passed a SPAR and a TESCO, two supermarkets prevalent in England, and I took a photo of them both and sent it to my mum and my sister. We walked a little more and I asked Chris if he had read the news and he said yes but to be honest there isn't really that much news, with which I concurred.

He got an alert to say that it was time to *Be Real* and that he should take a photo immediately so we looked around for something cool and Hungarian to be in the picture but there wasn't anything of significant beauty on that particular street so he took the photo of a soviet looking doorway on an old apartment building.

Then we walked a little further and I said out loud that I wanted to go in a TESCO, and then, lo and behold, literally one second later, another TESCO appeared right in front of us!

We drifted inside and I felt very excited.

It looked like a TESCO. It smelled like a TESCO. It had the same shelving units as in the UK and many of the same brands or products available there, but also many things that we do not have in England so that was very interesting. I haven't been to the UK for about six months so I felt like I was home. We reviewed the prices of various wines and tried to decipher the labels in Hungarian.

We were not yet comfortable with the currency conversion. The exchange rate was about 396 Hungarian forint to one euro. A bottle of wine for less than a thousand.

We didn't buy anything. We were just investigating. After that, we walked on towards the vegan place and saw a very ornate building that looked standard soviet from street level but extremely decorated with white and gold paint higher up. We wondered aloud about the religion here and I said I think some people are orthodox Christians? But I have no idea what that really means. Chris said they're probably secular now. And I said that there was a significant Jewish population here in the past, but presumably that isn't the case anymore.

At that moment, Chris asked me what is that big building over there? And I said I didn't know, but I had Google Maps open to try to find the vegan restaurant, so I cross-referenced and saw that it was, in fact, the Museum of the Country's Jewish History.

As we stood outside the vegan place looking at the menu, deciding if we wanted to go in, some German tourists stood behind us and started translating the menu from English into German out loud.

A few seconds later, some English tourists walked by, young women, and one of them said, *it's weird because if we were in England, everyone would be talking about it.*

The other one said, *she's not even dead yet.*
And a third said, *she probably is.*

I caught all this in the couple of seconds during which they passed us. Identified their regional accents.

We went into the restaurant, well it was more of a cafe really, and ordered a green falafel wrap and a bowl of truffle hummus to share. It was delicious. A perfect 4pm lunch.

The guy who was working there spoke fluent English.

We sheepishly said hello and thank you in Hungarian.

As I was eating, I had a realisation that propelled me to start writing this piece.

It just hit me.

The Queen is the ultimate woman with hat?!

It's literally what she's famous for.

2. Today is the day I'm supposed to have finished writing this book, by the way. My self-imposed deadline. But now it suddenly feels clear that there is something more to say.

After lunch, we walked around Budapest and pointed at things and remembered other times in our lives. It looks like Prague, we said. It looks like Bucharest. Looks like Zagreb. Like Berlin. I had visited Budapest once before, about fifteen years prior, with an old boyfriend one January. And though that trip had been disastrous (I wanted to break up), I remembered the city fondly, and wanted to come back under happier circumstances.

We saw the Danube, Buda castle, Fisherman's Bastion, and the magnificent Parliament building. Stood under a tree as a sun shower soaked the city.

As we walked along the river, I checked the news again and scrolled through the live updates on the BBC website. I said, *I don't understand what all the commotion is about. When people die, it usually takes a long time. Are we all just going to live in suspense indefinitely? It could be months!*

After all the excitement of TESCO, we were ecstatic once again upon finding a branch of DM, the drugstore chain prevalent in Germany.

We went inside and bought the same kind of toothpaste and the same kind of shampoo that we used to use when we lived in Berlin. I looked at all of the familiar products and read the familiar German vocabulary that my brain hasn't needed to use for a few years and I felt really good.

We walked back through the Jewish neighbourhood and pointed out interesting facets of the architecture. We passed a lot of cafes and ruin bars and restaurants that looked appealing and expressed interest in visiting them over the next week.

When we got back to our neighbourhood, we wanted to buy a few things for the evening and following morning, so we went to the SPAR.

The SPAR was not as nice as the TESCO, but it had everything that we needed. Bananas, yoghurt, biscuits, beers. I was walking around the shop carrying a two-litre bottle of water and a staff member stopped me and said *English*? I said *yes*. He said, *it's sparkling*, and I said, *that's great thank you.*

I debated buying a box of cereal and decided against it.

A Spanish family bounced around the shop and I listened to them discussing their plans. A couple of English people, much younger than me but still adults, walked in and selected some beers. I heard one of them say her brother had been making jokes in their family group chat, and that she thought it was too soon. *She's not even dead yet*, said her companion. *Well, she might be*, they laughed together.

When we went to pay, we once again sheepishly said hello in Hungarian. The young woman serving us said hello in English and asked us, *is this all*? We whispered to one another that we would probably need an extra bag and tried to figure out how to ask for this. In the meantime, the Spanish family appeared beside us in the line and the cashier turned to them and spoke quickly in Spanish. Chris said, *oh you speak Spanish too* (in Spanish) and she said, *I am Spanish* (in Spanish)! We laughed and proceeded to communicate with her in Spanish, suddenly feeling much more at ease.

As we walked back to the Airbnb, we remarked upon how funny it feels to be in a country where we don't know the language at all and how long it has been since this last happened to us. When people are speaking Hungarian with one another, I can't pick out a single word.

3. Back at the Airbnb I turned on BBC News. When you're outside of the UK, streaming is usually unavailable, but when something big happens, they give us access. To me, this has the same effect as going to TESCO. It feels like being home.

I lay on the bed with my laptop on my stomach and rested as the news anchors repeated themselves over and over. They kept saying that the Queen loved Balmoral and that the place was very important to her and then cutting to another person somewhere else who would say something very similar. I started to feel like I was going into a trance.

Nothing was happening at all.

I opened another tab on my computer and reread information about ruin bars and Hungarian street food. They have these things here called lángos, which are like deep-fried flatbreads covered in sour cream and cheese... and we needed to try them.

My phone vibrated on the bed beside me.

I picked it up and read a text from my sister on the lock screen. It said, 'the queen has died.' I wrote back, how do you know? And she texted me a photo of her TV screen, set to a different news channel, with a huge photo of the smiling monarch, and it said in big letters THE QUEEN DIES. My mum reacted with a thumbs down.

I wrote, I'm watching BBC news and they haven't announced it yet... but then a few seconds later they cut to a black screen and Huw Edwards appeared in a black tie and it seemed as though he repeated the same message three times but I was so shocked that I don't know if he really did or if I imagined that, and then they cut to a photo of the Queen and played the national anthem.

I was still just lying flat on the bed.

I looked over at Chris in disbelief.

It finally happened.

4. In the October 2001 issue of Rolling Stone magazine, David Foster Wallace's essay *The View from Mrs Thompson's* was first published, and it appeared with a note that said:

Location: *Bloomington, IL*
Dates: *11-13 Sept. 2001*
Subject: *Obvious*
Caveat: *Written very fast and in what probably qualifies as shock.*

Am I in shock? It's not exactly shocking for an old woman to die, and yet. Here we are, straddling historical eras. That night we went out to one of the ruin bars. Basically a big, neglected building with places to buy drinks on multiple floors, decorated with second hand furniture, different music and kitschy lighting in every room. A sprawling house party, immaculate ambiance, a lot of people who look like exchange students. We bought beers downstairs and kept walking upwards until we found a room that had somewhere available to sit. We found some bean bags in the middle of a room playing what I could only describe as experimental film, projected onto a graffitied wall. A DJ in the corner playing music that left absolutely no impression. I can't even pretend to describe it. All I really felt focused on was the light reflected from the disco ball spinning on the ceiling, going round and round. Making me feel still.

This isn't where I expected to be when it happened. But now this is what I'll always remember, always answer when somebody asks the question:

I was in Budapest.

CONVERSATIONALIST

A man in Brazil who loves the ocean and plans to sail around the world by himself. I ask him about his itinerary. First he will sail from Brazil to the Caribbean, at the end of the year, after the hurricane season. He will spend a few months there and then move onwards, across the Atlantic to Ireland, and then around the United Kingdom. After that, it's on to Germany where his brother lives, and then Holland, Belgium, France, Spain, Portugal, Spain again, and then he would need to wait for the right weather before he heads back across the Atlantic, through the Panama canal, and out into the Pacific, stopping at various islands, Hawaii, where he'll surf, French Polynesia, Easter Islands, Galapagos, I forget exactly, onto Asia, he's learning basic Japanese because he plans to stop there, and Mandarin for Taiwan, before he moves onto Indonesia, Australia, New Zealand, eventually he'll take on the longest nonstop portion of the journey, between the west coast of Australia and South Africa, when he can't stop at all because there will be pirates, and then from there, it's just onto St. Helena, in the middle of the South Atlantic before he goes home to Brazil. He is a dive master and a surfer. He will bring two surf boards and a stand-up paddle board. We talk about sharks. He says he likes them. But who knows if any of this is true.

A Sudanese man in Bucharest. He has been living there for four months and is having a difficult time because he can't find many people to speak English with. I tell him, in my experience, the young people in Romania can speak English very well but we agree that it might not be appropriate for him to approach teenagers on the street. He tells me that he struggles when he buys things in cafes or supermarkets, but he doesn't tend to go out much anyway because he is working all week. He is an electrical engineer. And on the weekends, he feels tired. He stays in 'the accommodation' and studies English and talks with his family on the phone. He is hoping to do a master's degree in an English-speaking country, like the UK or... the Netherlands. He tells me that Romania and Sudan had revolutions in the same year, 1991.

An Israeli man in Jerusalem who works at the controversially relocated American embassy tells me you can drive across the whole country in four hours and shows me the sunset out of his window. I can see the grand mosque against the pink-orange sky.

An Indian woman in Texas who recently got married and moved to Dallas where her husband is working. She can speak English very well but she wants to build her confidence. She doesn't feel comfortable speaking with people in America but she needs to because in six or seven more months, her working visa should be approved and then she wants to find a job. She doesn't care for American food, but she says she can find all of the ingredients she needs for cooking Indian recipes because there are many Indian people in Dallas. Little India, she says, smiling.

A Turkish woman in Istanbul who wants to move to Belgium to do a master's in fine art. She says she specialises in textiles, specifically knitting. I tell her I do embroidery. We coo at each other about working with soft fabrics.

A Japanese man who teaches economics and accounting at a small university in a small city in Japan. He wants to practise English because he doesn't feel very confident and he has noticed that when he tries sometimes, his eyebrows start to twitch. As he says this, he motions towards his twitching eyebrows and tells me, 'Like this!' We talk a little about writing. He is working on a 6000-word research paper. He asks me how many words I write per day. I tell him it's not really like that. He asks if I'm an introvert or an extrovert. I tell him I like long periods of solitude. He says he agrees.

An Egyptian man who lives in Dubai for work. He tells me that he went to a school run by French monks, and when I express surprise he asks me why? I tell him I didn't know that there were French monks in Egypt and he abruptly informs me that he is a Christian. He says that 85% of Egyptians are Muslim, but around 15% are Christian. I say, okay. He has visited the UK before and went to London, Liverpool and Edinburgh. I ask if he is a Liverpool fan and he laughs and says yes. He asks me if I know about Mohamed Salah, 'the Egyptian king' and I laugh and say yes. We talk about running and he says that he often goes to the 2km track near his house late in the evenings this time of year. Even if the temperature is high, say 36 degrees, he can still run comfortably, so long as he is not in direct sunlight.

A man from Hong Kong wearing a Manchester United shirt who asks me to go through the list of 2022/23 Premier League teams and correct his pronunciation. He struggles with Fulham, Everton, Nottingham Forest, Brighton & Hove Albion, Tottenham Hotspur, and Crystal Palace.

A Turkish man in Istanbul who also wants to talk about the Premier League. He had applied for a tourist visa to visit the UK last year and was denied. I ask him why and he says he doesn't know. He says he works for the tax office. He says it is his dream to go and see Liverpool play at Anfield and that he will never give up. We talk about the World Cup in Qatar, and he says he is not excited. He says the Saudis want to buy all of football. He says that inflation in Turkey is at 80%. He says next year there is an election and he hopes the government will be thrown out. He says the older people in Turkey are not educated and have kept them in power for twenty-one years, but the younger generation are very smart, so something's got to give.

WOMAN WITH HAT 5

1. I lie on the beach and type into the notes app what will soon become the concluding piece of writing in the book I have been working on all year. The famously self-referential, WOMAN WITH HAT.

2. It is October 2nd, 2022.

3. I will be thirty-five years old next week and this is what I am doing with my life.

4. Which is very lucky.

5. It wasn't the reception of WOMAN WITH HAT that changed the course of art history. (The painting, I mean, this time.)

6. It was something within Henri Matisse that allowed him to paint what he really wanted to paint.

7. Something that I can feel right now and need to hold on to.

Thank you to the writers I collaborated with on this book: Oscar Wilde, Rachelle Toarmino & Ashley Obscura. Thank you to Sebastian Castillo for exchanging manuscripts and insight. Thank you to Sarah and Gabby and Rachael and Maggie and Meggie and Karina and Luna and Sheila and Kate, in general. Thank you to the poetry book club for prompting some of these pieces. Thank you to Chris for all the conversations at dinner. Thank you to everyone I wrote about. I hope you don't mind.

On November 7th, 2022, a stage adaptation of this book, also written by me, was performed at the Kraine Theater in New York City, which is kind of ridiculous, I know. Thank you to Jordan Debor, Oscar d'Artois, and Gabby Bess for starring in this production alongside me. (A revival of the original *Lady Windermere's Fan Club* cast!) And to Peter BD for being the double in our theatrical double-feature.

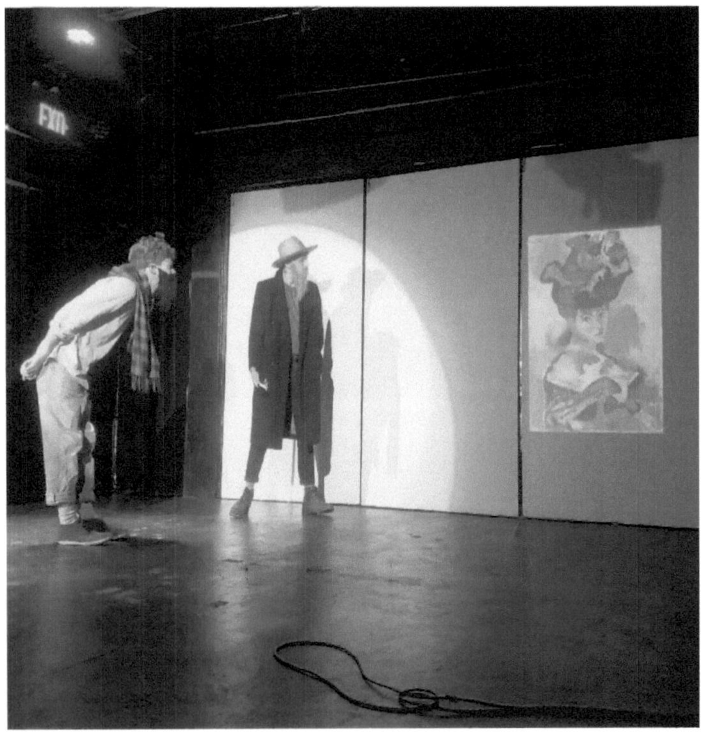

Scenes from Woman with Hat, the play.

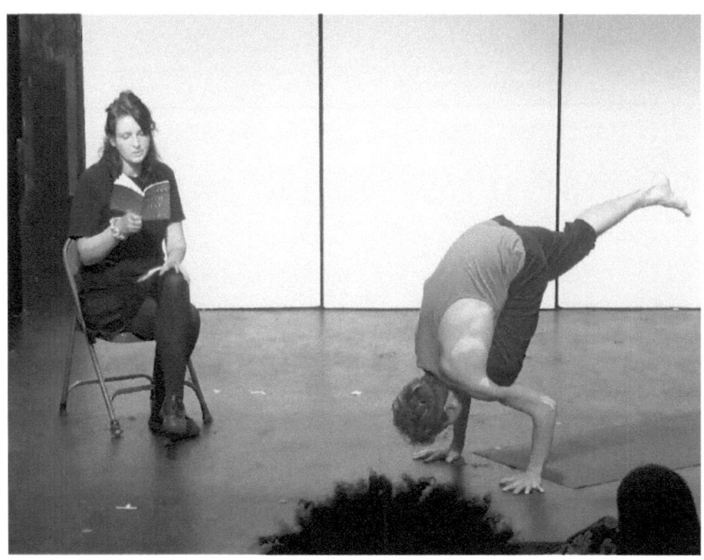

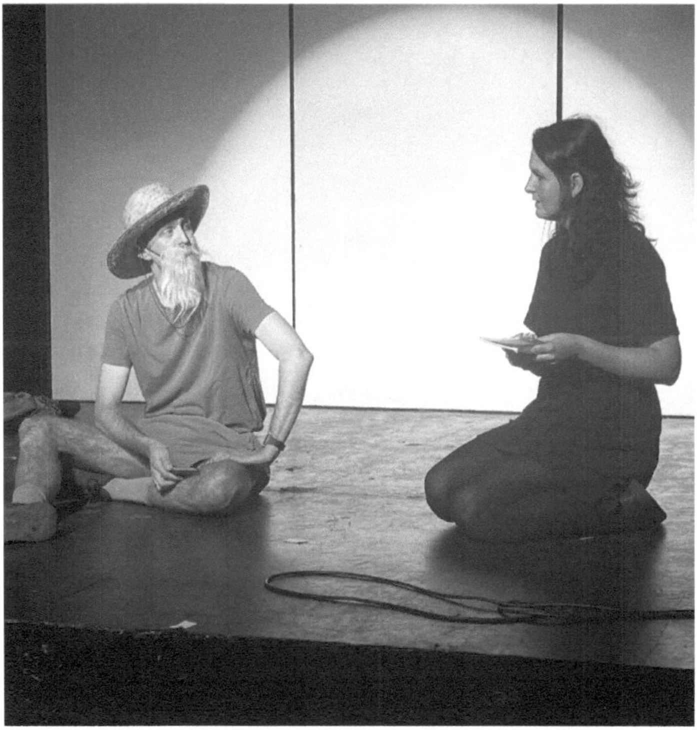

The play is about a woman visited by the spirit of Henri Matisse while trying to finish a book inspired by his work.

As an épilogue, here is the script for the opening scene.

MY THEATRICAL DEBUT

THE PERSONS OF THE PLAY

CHRIS: Prevalent Contemporary Art Critic

JORDAN: Henry Matisse

LUCY: Herself

SCENE 1. AN OFF-BROADWAY THEATRE,

NOVEMBER 2022

The action of the scene takes place at the Salon d'Automne,

in Paris, 1905.

Narrator: *(Peter in the sound booth)* WOMAN WITH HAT by Lucy K Shaw

The lights come up and classic French accordion music begins to play.

The painting WOMAN WITH HAT by Henri Matisse is projected onto the back wall.

Narrator: *(speaking slowly)* 1905, Paris, France.

Two men (Jordan and Chris) walk out from stage left and begin circling each other silently while studying the painting. Jordan is wearing a trench coat, a long, fake, grey beard, and a wide brimmed hat. Chris is wearing a button-down shirt with a scarf and a long, fake, black beard.

Lucy sits in the front row with the rest of the audience, unable to believe that she has gotten herself into this situation, nervous at the possibility that her first play could be a catastrophe, but excited to take her place on stage in the subsequent scenes.

Music fades out. The men stand side by side in front of the painting.

Chris/PCAC: (with a very thick French accent) I hate this painting! It is so... ugly.

Jordan/Henri Matisse: (in his natural Australian accent) Hey, that's my wife!

Chris/PCAC: Oh, you are the artist? I didn't know.

Jordan/Henri Matisse: Yes... My name is Henri Matisse. *(Pronounced Henry.)*

Chris/PCAC: Hello Henri. My name is Prevalent Contemporary Art Critic.

Jordan/Henri Matisse: Oh goddammit. Well, what's your problem?

Chris/PCAC: Your painting is... a piece of trash.

Jordan/Henri Matisse: (dramatically) Rude!

Chris/PCAC: The colours... they are not representative of reality...

Jordan/Henri Matisse: They represent what I feel!

Chris/PCAC: You feel like your wife is green?

Jordan/Henri Matisse: Sometimes...

Chris/PCAC: How can you bring this piece of shit painting to the prestigious *salon d'automne*? How can you call this art? You are insulting me!

Jordan/Henri Matisse: No, actually I would love to do that, but that's not what...

Chris/PCAC: You have flung a pot of paint in the face of the public! Everybody here hates your painting!!! *(gestures to the audience who begin to boo)*

Jordan/Henri Matisse: Listen, I don't really care what you think. I don't paint for you. I don't paint for anybody. Creativity takes courage! And I paint from within! From the moment I held the box of colours in my hands, I knew this was my life. I threw myself into it like a beast that plunges towards the thing it loves.

Chris/PCAC: You... what?

Jordan/Henri Matisse: The importance of an artist is to be measured by the quantity of new signs which he has introduced to the language of art.

Chris/PCAC: Interesting theory but incorrect.

Jordan/Henri Matisse: An artist should never be a prisoner of themselves, prisoner of style, prisoner of reputation, prisoner of success...

Chris/PCAC: Bla bla bla, whatever. Now please tell me, what is the name of this painting so that I can mention it unfavourably in my very important review of this show which will surely send your career into a nosedive!?

Jordan/Henri Matisse: This painting is called.... *(long dramatic pause)*... WOMAN WITH HAT!

Chris/PCAC: (typing on phone) Woman...with...hat... Okay then. Thank you for your help. *(starts walking away)* I bid you good day!

Jordan/Henri Matisse: Hey, Prevalent Contemporary Art Critic

Chris/PCAC: Yes, Henri Matisse.

Jordan/Henri Matisse: *flings a pot of paint over him* Good day!

French accordion music resumes as the pot of paint is flung and they both exit stage right.

Lucy K Shaw wrote WOMAN WITH HAT, Troisième Vague, How to be a Perfect Bride, WAVES & The Motion.

For the secret liner notes to this book, visit:
shabbydollhouse.com/wwh

ALSO FROM

SHABBY DOLL HOUSE

WE DIE IN ITALY

by Sarah Jean Alexander

TROISIÈME VAGUE

by Lucy K Shaw

COMING SOON...

SALMON

by Sebastian Castillo

THE MOAN WILDS

by Caroline Rayner

www.ingramcontent.com/pod-product-compliance
Ingram Content Group UK Ltd.
Pitfield, Milton Keynes, MK11 3LW, UK
UKHW041956190726
13854UKWH00005B/2000

9 781737 924227